The often quoted saying "When the student is
pear" holds true in this recent work of Dr. Harry
of Jesus Christ is thoroughly enmeshed in one moral crisis after the other,
and we have been in desperate need for a truly biblical answer to this crisis. Several thousand years ago, Job observed that ". . . Increased years
should teach wisdom." It is evident that Dr. Schaumburg's years of experience and his commitment to a thoroughly biblical approach to dealing with
this issue has produced a work that shines with penetrating light into the
one of the darkest areas of 21st century Christian life. I commend this work
as a handbook for study in every church, as a resource to every pastor who
has or will face this matter in their ministry and as a diagnostic tool for
personal evaluation of one's own life and walk. No pastor's library should
be without this wonderful tool. If *Undefiled* is taken seriously, it could produce a sea change in Christian behavior.

Bishop Joseph L. Garlington, Sr.
Reconciliation Ministries International

As the church awakens to the mushrooming challenges of sexual sin and
temptation, this book is important. Not only does Dr. Schaumburg capture
hearts through compelling narrative, he addresses the real issues head on.
The author integrates a much needed biblical view of sex into the fabric of
everyday faith. But most importantly, Dr. Schaumburg emphasizes the concept of sin, rather than the more typical categorization of sexual sin as disease. Because sin is thoroughly addressed here with the gospel of Jesus
Christ, hope and power are present. *Undefiled* is substantial, but written in
a way that people can comprehend. It is my prayer that this work will be
widely read—leading to understanding, repentance, and faith, and God's
blessing for people and families.

Joseph Wheat
Pastor, PCA

From a former client:

Before going to see Dr. Schaumburg, I was terrified. Not only had my world as I thought I knew it crumbled, but I was desperate for some answers to why my spouse had done these things: didn't he care about our marriage? Our family? What was so wrong with me that he had to go elsewhere? While reeling from the revelations, I faced the thought of what to do next: should we spend more money we didn't have on counseling that although was "Christian" hadn't helped in the past?

Now, as an alumni of Dr. Schaumberg's method, I can tell you that this book offers a real answer for the above questions facing so many broken marriages today. The real solution is not about the counseling, the recovery programs, and finding who to blame for one's behavior—we tried those and they didn't bring true change. Dr. Schaumberg's method gets to the heart of the matter, literally. He guides each person to examine their own heart and see how it lines up with God's will for their life, step by step, just as if you were going through his program. You will not be the same person you were if you read and follow the instructions in this book; in it you will find the keys to sexual redemption.

From a former client:

The resources Harry is making available to use in the local church will transform people's hearts and minds. I am confident that the truth contained in these new resources will begin to shatter the strongholds that have held many captive for years. If more people are exposed to this truth, hopefully the tide of self-help can be stemmed and the tide of clean heart, clean mind can begin to grow.

Undefiled

Redemption from Sexual Sin,
Restoration for Broken Relationships

HARRY SCHAUMBURG

MOODY PUBLISHERS
CHICAGO

All Scripture quotations, unless otherwise indicated, are taken from *The Holy Bible, English Standard Version*. Copyright © 2000, 2001 by Crossway Bibles, a division of Good News Publishers. Used by permission. All rights reserved.

Scripture quotations marked NIV are taken from the *Holy Bible, New International Version®*. NIV®. Copyright © 1973, 1978, 1984 by International Bible Society. Used by permission of Zondervan. All rights reserved.

Scripture quotations marked KJV are taken from the King James Version.

All italics added to Scripture are the author's.

All Web sites listed herein are accurate at the time of publication, but may change in the future or cease to exist. The listing of Web site references and resources does not imply publisher endorsement of the site's entire contents. Groups, corporations, and organizations are listed for informational purposes, and listing does not imply publisher endorsement of their activities.

Editor: Christopher Reese
Interior Design: David Laplaca/debestdesignco.
Cover Design: The DesignWorks Group (www.thedesignworksgroup.com)
Cover Image: Corbis (#42-16776770)

Library of Congress Cataloging-in-Publication Data

Schaumburg, Harry W.
    Undefiled : redemption from sexual sin, restoration for broken relationships / Harry W. Schaumburg.
        p. cm.
    Includes bibliographical references.
    ISBN 978-0-8024-6069-1
    1. Sex—Religious aspects—Christianity. I. Title.
BT708.S29 2009
241'.66—dc22

                                                                2009014692

This book is printed on acid free recycled paper containing 30% PCW (Post Consumer Waste) and manufactured in the United States of America by Bethany Press.

We hope you enjoy this book from Moody Publishers. Our goal is to provide high-quality, thought-provoking books and products that connect truth to your real needs and challenges. For more information on other books and products written and produced from a biblical perspective, go to www.moodypublishers.com or write to:

Moody Publishers
820 N. LaSalle Boulevard
Chicago, IL 60610

1 3 5 7 9 10 8 6 4 2

Printed in the United States of America

To Rosemary,
with all my love

*When I see you, when I'm with you, when I touch you,
my life and my soul find the greatest earthly joy.*

Contents

*Let marriage be held in honor among all,
and let the marriage bed be undefiled.*
—Hebrews 13:4

Introduction

Here are only a few of the many situations that need sexual redemption:

- You feel very alone in a marriage that has little satisfying intimacy
- Your husband treats you like a sexual toy or object
- Your wife has little interest in sexual intimacy
- You suspect that your mate is involved emotionally and/or physically with another person
- You cannot stop indulging in shameful sexual habits, such as Internet pornography, sex chats, frequent masturbation, or other disturbing activities

This book has two purposes. First, I want to present information based on Scripture and my counseling experience that will help you distinguish what is true and what is false in contemporary thinking about sexuality. Second, I want to guide you through a process of redemption that will help you face your sexual problems with courage, power, and spiritual insight. This process will take time as you progress through each chapter. The first eight chapters are important as they provide you with a foundation necessary for lasting change, a vital apprehension of the real problem, and practical resources for understanding and helping others. If you feel impatient, remember that this investment will pay off in the long run when you reach the later chapters.

Each chapter begins with a short excerpt from *The Valley of Vision: A*

Collection of Puritan Prayers and Devotions. May God use their words to soften your heart for what you read. At the end of each chapter, I have written several questions for reflection designed to help you interact with the material and apply it to your own life.

This book is an attempt to build on the sound doctrines of Scripture, but is not a theological textbook. The theological questions that relate to some of the issues under discussion have been addressed by many competent evangelical writers, and I encourage you to seek out those resources for further reading and study.

After thirty years of working closely with well over three thousand people struggling to make sense of sexual problems, I believe that there is only one meaningful and lasting solution—the one I seek to present in this book—sexual redemption.

CHAPTER ONE

Sexual Redemption?

Give me to view a discovered sinfulness.
To know that though my sins are crucified
they are never wholly mortified.[1]

How did sex become such a problem for so many?

My ministry is with people struggling with issues related to sexuality. Although many of them find me because they are in crisis, their challenges, desires, hopes, and experiences are much like yours and mine. It is not easy to satisfy our desires. Just when our dreams are satisfied, we often wake up in a nightmare, or the perception that something is still missing.

I want you to meet a couple in trouble because of sex. Their story illustrates that these are not the best of times in the sexual arena. We desperately need sexual redemption.

My introduction to Carrie and Jim (not their actual names) came via a telephone call to my office in Colorado on a sparkling fall afternoon. Carrie was articulate and thoughtful, but obviously crushed as she haltingly, with tearful sniffs, explained why she was contacting me. Her story resembled many others I've heard. "Dr. Schaumburg," she began, "I got your name from Focus on the Family—can you help us?"

Like many wives today, Carrie was concerned about the lack of passion and intimacy in her marriage. Suspicious, she had checked Jim's laptop and found many recent visits to pornographic websites.

"Please understand," Carrie continued, "we're both Christians! My husband is loved and admired by our children and everyone who knows him. He is a good man!"

She paused, her voice choking. "What is going on here? I've awakened to a nightmare, Dr. Schaumburg. This is not the man I married! I don't know what to do, but I can't live like this. Can you help?"

Before answering her question, I asked Carrie to fill in some details on herself and Jim. They had met over thirty years ago at college, fallen in love, married, and borne three children—two boys and a girl. Active in their church, they were coleaders of a couples group that met for Bible study and fellowship. Invariably, at least one couple in the group was struggling in their marriage and Carrie and Jim provided counsel.

When a wife like Carrie discovers unfaithfulness, either heart adultery or physical adultery, meaningful solutions seem impossible. I continued our conversation. "Carrie, this may be the darkest moment of your life. Jim has betrayed you at a level that seems to tear away every good moment and memory you have of your relationship. The enormity of his sin must be faced head-on. Believe me, in all this mess, God is at work. Yes, the problem is very serious, and I know this sounds impossible right now, but there is hope."

"Dr. Schaumburg, that sounds good, but I don't know what to think now."

I offered my sympathy to Carrie and briefly explained how couples come to our counseling workshop for about a week of intensive education and counseling. "Do you think that Jim would come with you for intensive counseling?" I asked.

"Jim is such a private and proud man! I don't even know how to confront him about all this so we can get the help we need! He has never been willing to go to any counseling—I've begged him!"

Carrie went on and told me of the confusing contradiction between Jim's involvement with Internet pornography and his Christian reputation. "I just don't get it. He's a good father and we're leaders in our church. I feel like I don't know who this man is anymore!"

"I know your trust has been shattered, but let your heart speak gently and softly," I replied. "He is your husband, the father of your children. He needs you now more than ever. Don't run from the pain. All attempts to kill the pain will only lead to greater and greater pain."

Carrie didn't speak. All I heard was her sniffling on the other end.

"When Jim comes home tonight," I went on, "pour out your heart to him, both the hurt you feel and the concern you have for him and your marriage. Invite him to come with you to our intensive counseling program. If he has any questions, have him call me."

"Okay, Dr. Schaumburg. I'll try." As Carrie and I said good-bye, I encouraged her to call me soon and let me know what happened.

Carrie did call back several days later. There were no tears this time, just hard anger.

"Dr. Schaumburg, I kicked him out of the house! I did what you said. When he couldn't deny the evidence, he confessed, but there was no brokenness! He blamed me for not having interest in sex. He said it was all my fault! When he said that, I blew up and we started shouting. It was terrible! I slept on the couch. The next morning he was different and admitted he'd had a problem with pornography and masturbation since he was eleven. This is unbelievable!"

"I'm sorry this is so hard," I said.

"He has lied to me, and I still don't know if there is more he hasn't told me. I can't stand to be around him. My married daughter is furious and says I should divorce him. I don't know if I did the right thing when I asked him to get out. What am I going to do?"

"Is there any chance the two of you can come for help?"

"Oh, Dr. Schaumburg, I forgot to tell you that! He did say he would consider coming to your workshop. When could we come for your intensive counseling?"

I told her we had no openings for two months. She was disappointed but agreed that the wait would be worthwhile. Little did we know there was more pain to come.

As this book progresses, I will relate Jim and Carrie's story and the process of healing that eventually occurred for them as individuals, as well as in their marriage.

Obviously, the personalities, particular issues, and experience of every person differ. The spiritual maturity of the individuals, and their receptivity to biblical truth and to any wisdom I might offer, are never exactly the same. However, I have found in over two decades of counseling with more than three thousand people that the sexual redemption that Carrie and Jim eventually experienced is available to anyone—any person—who allows God's beautiful restoration process to unfold.

While we live in a sexually explicit society, in counseling I find many who are uninformed about sex, struggle with sexual dissatisfaction,[2] and are sexually dysfunctional.[3] I concluded long ago that the complexity of our sexual functioning is beyond our comprehension. First, we must marvel at God's design and second, with gratitude, be amazed at the Father's heart for sex. God has placed more nerve endings in the penis and clitoris than any other part of the body except the tongue. Clearly, God wants us to enjoy the pleasure of good food and holy sex.

There's a wide range of issues surrounding sexual intimacy, which are revealed by comments like these that I've heard countless times:

Woman: "We have no intimacy in our marriage. Neither did my parents, but I refuse to live like this."

Man: "Throughout my married life I've been very selfish. My wife has never had my heart, and in our sexual relationship, she often feels like an object. Given such a poor relational history, there's so little for my wife to look back to as a basis upon which to rebuild our marriage."

Woman: "I want to be looked at and to feel good about myself. I just like looking hot when I go out. It makes me feel powerful around men."

Man: "I have attended some popular seminars on sexual addiction and read some books, but little has changed."

Woman: "Men are such losers—it's all about sex. So just forget it! Besides, Jesus is my lover."

Man: "She tells me I'm stupid and can't do anything right. I feel like a child; I get no respect."

Woman: "My grandson is twelve and looking at pornography on the Internet. It just breaks my heart. Where will this end?"

Man: "I've not been supportive as we have begun to struggle through this mess. At times I've dragged my heels about going for counseling and asking for help."

Woman: "When the affair started, it wasn't about sex. We were just good friends—I need that given the distance in my marriage. We started kissing and one thing led to another. Now I can't imagine losing him."

Man: "Last night we agreed that I should move out. This morning, for some reason, she's agreed to try again."

Woman: "If it was another woman, I could deal with this. But a *man*? What do I tell the children?"

Man: "I continued to lie to her and denied there was a problem. I tried in my foolishness to get her to see that it is her problem, because looking at some porn was not that big a deal and she just needed to get over it."

Woman: "If only he would take some responsibility in this family. How can I respect him? I feel like his mother."

Behind each of these statements there is a real man or woman expressing themselves sexually and spiritually.

I know in my own experience, and from hearing story after story in my counseling office, that there is sexual brokenness and sin in each of us. But this reality often is not apparent.

For example, consider a good-looking couple named John and Kathy who had been sexually active in previous dating relationships, but when they met were determined to maintain some semblance of purity until their wedding night. For their honeymoon they booked via the Internet a secluded cabin in the mountains of Colorado. Full of anticipation and love, at 1 a.m. on their wedding night, they arrived at the cabin and found it rat infested. Exhausted, and faced with a five-hour drive to the nearest hotel, they decided to stay but spent a sleepless night with little sexual interest. The next day they drove to a four-star hotel with clean sheets, but Kathy had developed a yeast infection that made sexual intimacy painful. John, clean from what many would consider harmless masturbation[4] since he'd met Kathy, in frustration immediately returned to his old self-comfort and withdrew from his bride.

Six months passed and John and Kathy still looked like the perfect couple, but inside their sexually dysfunctional relationship, they were desperate for help. Their circumstances differed, but like Jim and Carrie, they needed sexual redemption.

After nearly three decades of helping individuals and couples, and based on a continual study of the Bible, I've reached this conclusion: *To be spiritually mature, you must be sexually mature; to be sexually mature, you must be spiritually mature.* That in brief is the message of this book and the essence of sexual redemption.

Sexual redemption involves more than resolution of sexual problems and challenges. For example, most Christian couples know that God designed fulfilling sex for marriage but many fail to experience it. Trying "seven tips to enhance your love life" may bring some excitement but there's more to sexuality than romantic techniques. Sexual redemption is larger than a fulfilling sex life in marriage.

And how might sexual redemption relate to childhood sexual abuse? I started my counseling career working with incestuous families and since then have counseled hundreds of men and women sexually abused as children. The violation of another person sexually is very harmful. Forgiving your abuser is an important first step, but there is more to understanding our fragile sexuality than that.

Sexual redemption takes us beyond the healing of past wounds and calls us to glorify God spiritually and sexually.

Sexual redemption also addresses any clinging shame related to premarital sex. Of those three thousand social histories I mentioned, 40 percent were in full-time Christian work. Yet I estimate conservatively that less than 20 percent were virgins when they married.

Remaining a virgin until marriage, a practice all but lost within the church, is still God's standard. But being a virgin or a "technical virgin" on your wedding night isn't all that God intends. Sexual redemption is living spiritually and sexually for a purpose other than a self-seeking agenda.

Pastor and author John Piper makes two crucial points on sexuality:

> The first is that sexuality is designed by God as a way to know God in Christ more fully. And the second is that knowing God in Christ more fully is designed as a way of guarding and guiding our sexuality. Now to state the two points again, this time negatively, in the first place all misuses of our sexuality distort the true knowledge of Christ. And, in the second place, all misuses of our sexuality derive from not having the true knowledge of Christ.[5]

The way we handle our sexuality and spirituality is meant to show the supremacy of Christ. We know—or we should know—that this is true, but do we really understand it and own it in our hearts? Every person is a sexual being, created in the image of God. Now that sounds inviting, but the truth is we also are all fallen sinners. If we separate our sexuality and spirituality into different compartments, we not only diminish our sexual beauty, our sexual purity, and our sexual meaning but also our very soul. Our soul and our sexuality are profoundly connected, and yet we have lost this correlation between knowing Christ and sexual wholeness.

Knowing Christ is to govern *all* of our sexuality and *all* of our spirituality in a way that expresses the image of God and demonstrates that we are walking worthy of our calling. The loss of holy spirituality and holy sexuality brings into question our sexual redemption and whether we know God as we should.

This book is about a full sexuality and a full spirituality that can only be found by finding satisfaction in God and God alone. This book is also about dedicating your sexuality, your spirituality, your life—*all* for His highest. Sexual redemption begins at the cross, is rooted in a change of heart, and is lived out in a relationship before and after two sinners say "I do."

One question you may have at this point is, "But if my spouse and I can't come to Colorado for an intensive counseling experience, is there any hope for us?"

Yes, most definitely! We have had significant success with couples coming for intensive counseling, but there is no magic in that experience, either. What ultimately "works" is a combination of learning the truth and a commitment to walk through the process of repentance, forgiveness, and sexual redemption that God orchestrates. You can do this no matter where you live and what you have been through. The answers are in God's Word and in His desire to heal the brokenhearted and reclaim lost and hopeless sinners, which quite frankly are all of us.

This book outlines the same process that individuals and couples go through who participate in our intensive counseling program.[6] More than anything, what needs to happen is for each participant to understand the truth about their sexuality. This book in significant ways parallels the truth encounter that occurs during Biblical Intensive Counseling, which for many people is a fresh way of looking at life and their situation. I do not spend countless hours counseling. What I do is guide a process, which the individuals accomplish for the most part without me—one-on-one with God and their spouse.

I say this to defuse the idea that the only way the principles in this book will work is to spend a week in a remote location working with a "high-powered therapist." That's not it—believe me, I know! I have no magic potion. I do have God's Word and His willing and powerful involvement in the healing process. Besides, much of the important work in experiencing sexual redemption continues *after* a couple leaves the intensive program.

There's no shortcut through the process of acknowledging sin and experiencing redemption. But there's also no need to think that the process will take years before true change begins! No follower of Christ ever has to say about any problem, "I guess I will always be an addict or trapped in bondage to sin." No, no, no, no! That is not the message of the gospel.

Let God work. Regardless of how you got to where you are, don't limit

God now because of your fears. Your marriage may be hanging by a thread. I know you may be thinking, *We've tried everything and nothing has worked. Why should this be any different? Nothing is going to change!* All I ask is that you not limit God. He cares and I can tell you that I have seen incredibly real, lasting change in many, many couples.

Take Lisa and Steve, for example. Their story is unusual but demonstrates so clearly what God can accomplish. Unknown to Lisa, Steve had struggled with homosexuality for years. They married but never—not once—had sexual intercourse. Eventually Steve's issue was exposed when he initiated a sexual relationship with an underage young man. He was convicted and sent to prison. Steve lost almost everything in the process, but Lisa stuck with him during his nearly five-year incarceration.

Before Steve's release from prison, Lisa contacted our office and arranged for the two of them to attend one of our sessions. By the time Lisa and Steve arrived, they had been married for fifteen years. I know this may seem hard to believe, but during all those years they'd still never had sex.

Their intensive counseling time went well. God intervened in their life and marriage, and while they were still participating in the program, the two finally consummated their marriage by having sex for the first time. The day after this momentous event, when they arrived in my office for a visit, I don't think I've ever seen two people who were both so startled and happy at the same time! We praised God together. What we did not know then is that during this first time of intimacy, Lisa had conceived their first child. You now know why I need no convincing that with God "all things are possible"!

And here's the icing on the cake: Every year I still get a Christmas card from this family, and their growing daughter is a reminder of the unique sexual redemption this couple experienced through God's grace.

If in a week God can change the course of that kind of personal and relational history, what might He have in store for you?

A fundamental principle of this book is that in all the evil that sexual sin brings into a life or a marriage, we must never doubt God's love and His purifying discipline. What was true long ago for Joseph in the wake of his horrible betrayal by his brothers is true in all cases of unfaithfulness: "As for you, you meant evil against me, but God meant it for good" (Genesis 50:20).

I often run into couples several years after their experience of BIC. Frequently, the wife takes me aside to whisper in my ear, "Dr. Schaumburg. He really is a different man!"

Please hear me clearly on this: There is hope. It is hope based in truth and the power of God. You too can experience sexual redemption.

The Path to Sexual Redemption

1 What similarities, if any, do you find between Jim and Carrie's story and your own?

2 Is there sexual dissatisfaction or sexual dysfunction in your marriage? If so, do you have the courage to face the problem with your spouse? If not, why?

3 Do you agree or disagree with the statement, *To be spiritually mature, you must be sexually mature; to be sexually mature, you must be spiritually mature?* Why do you agree or disagree?

4 What sexual redemption would you like to see in your life and marriage?

CHAPTER TWO

Revealing the Darkness

If I behold beauty it is a bait to lust . . .
Keep me ever mindful of my natural state,
but let me not forget heavenly title,
or the grace that can deal with every sin.[1]

A month after my last conversation with Carrie, I received a frantic message on my answering machine from Jim. "Dr. Schaumburg, you don't know me, but this is Carrie's husband, Jim. I've got to talk to you! Carrie is threatening to divorce me and is refusing to come for counseling."

I called Jim back immediately. He was in a panic. He explained that in spite of all their problems, he loved Carrie. "I've been a fool, Dr. Schaumburg. Carrie did some more checking on my computer and found out that the pornography wasn't the only problem."

"Oh, really . . . ," I answered.

"I've been chatting online with three or four different women and emailed two of them. Carrie read the emails. There's a lot of sexual stuff in them. I can't believe I've been so stupid. What do I do? She's now refusing to come to Biblical Intensive Counseling and threatening to talk to an attorney. I think my marriage is over, Dr. Schaumburg."

Sadly, I have too many conversations like this. Pornography, and the behaviors it tends to encourage, is a plague in our society—and I fear the worst is yet to come. Because of the proliferation of porn, especially via the Internet, some variation of Jim's story could be told by millions of men, and increasingly, by women as well.

I'll share more about what I told Jim later, but I think it's appropriate, before we explore the path to sexual redemption, to understand how badly we need it. Whether you are the person in bondage to sexual sin, the spouse of a sexual sinner, or an elder called to help, in this chapter I want to look at some statistics and other indicators that reveal what has gone wrong related to our sexuality. Later chapters will further our understanding.

Dark Days

Almost twenty years ago, about the time I was writing a book on false intimacy, my first book from a biblical perspective on sexual addiction, it seemed like everyone was clueless that so many people were struggling with their sexuality. I would tell someone I was writing a book on "sexual addiction" and the response was, "Sexual what?" No one would ask that question today. We live in a dark time where it is nearly impossible to escape sexual temptation, dissatisfaction, dysfunction, and perversion.

The list of indicators that there is a massive problem is long and varied: Premarital sex; promiscuity; sexual dysfunction; sexual dissatisfaction; unfulfilled relational needs; the divorce rate; confused gender roles;[2] increased acceptance of homosexuality; gay marriage; bisexuality; gender identity issues; ineffective male leadership; radical feminism; male bashing; female objectifying; immodesty;[3] sex in advertising;[4] pornography; child pornography; physical adultery; heart adultery; hooking up; exhibitionism; voyeurism; prostitution; sex tourism; rape; incest; and more.

Of course, the problems caused by pornography get much of the attention, and rightly so, because porn is often in the mix with most sex-related problems. Think about it: twenty-four hours a day, year-round, worldwide, $3,075.63 is spent on pornography *every second!*[5] The total number of users that look at pornography on the Internet every second is 28,258. Every thirty-nine minutes a new pornographic video is created[6] in the United States.[7]

In 2006, worldwide revenues for pornography were estimated at $97 billion, a total that exceeds the combined revenues of Microsoft, Google, Amazon, eBay, Yahoo!, Apple, Netflix, and Earthlink! China leads the world in pornography, spending $27.4 billion, followed by South Korea at $25.7 billion, and Japan with $20 billion. The United States is fourth with $13.3 billion.[8] Unfortunately, such numbers only begin to indicate the cataclysmic personal and spiritual cost to individuals, marriages, families, children, churches, and communities. The sheer frequency at which men (or for that matter, women) look at other human beings with lustful intent is a powerful indicator that something is drastically wrong sexually and spiritually.

Here are more alarming statistics related to the Internet: a reputable, comprehensive report indicates that in just one year, between 2005 and 2006, these changes occurred in the use of keyword searches:

- 622 percent increase in searches for "adult dating"
- 382 percent increase in searches for "sex ads"
- 301 percent increase in searches for "adult sex"[9]

Pornography via the Internet has gained a stranglehold on American culture, but for years we have assumed it's an adult male problem. Statistics[10] seem to signal a disturbing new trend: pornography is no longer strictly a male problem. In 2006, there were over seventy-five million search requests using the word "sex"—50 percent were by men, and 50 percent by women. Of the over thirty million searches for "adult dating," 36 percent were men, and 64 percent were women. For the 13,982,729 searches of "teen sex," 44 percent were men, 56 percent women. And for the over thirteen million search requests for "adult sex," 36 percent were men, 64 percent were women. If interest in pornography is growing significantly among women, how will that further weaken marriages and further pollute the spiritual life of the church?

Another disturbing development that must concern parents is that approximately 20 percent of those using these four keywords in Internet searches were children under age the age of eighteen. Another 20 percent were young men and women between the ages of eighteen and twenty-four.[11] Even more sobering is the data reporting that 90 percent of eight- to sixteen-year-olds have viewed pornography online, with eleven being the average age of a child's first Internet exposure to pornography. Between the ages of fifteen and seventeen, 80 percent of children have had multiple hard-core exposures.[12] If children were not able to be online, the vast majority of them would not be exposed to porn. In the world of the Internet, boys and girls are still looking for information on sex; but in this generation of children, sex is now looking for them.

The cell phone is the newest "delivery system" for pornography, an area of porn business that's expected to reach $1.5 billion in Europe in 2012. No doubt America will not be far behind.[13] While speaking in Mexico in the spring of 2008, I learned the middle school students there were using their cell phones to take nude pictures of each other and post them on the Internet.

Widespread private access to the Internet has largely contributed to the above-mentioned numbers. Even ten to fifteen years ago, social and religious stigmas limited sex-video rentals or porn-magazine purchases. The Internet's offer of complete anonymity and instant accessibility has changed everything. When Internet pornography first became the preferred form of lust, most people were not aware that they left a history of websites visited. I have counseled hundreds who were caught in sexual sin without realizing how vulnerable they were to being caught. I believe God used their ignorance so they could get help. However, software for erasing these tracks is now widely available, and the feature (aptly nicknamed "Porn Mode") is also included in the newest release of Microsoft's Internet Explorer. History can be erased, and the secrecy hidden deep in the hearts and lives of countless children, teenagers, and adults will damage more lives, spiritually and sexually.

Sex tourism and trafficking has long been in our history, but while writing this chapter, I was horrified to read in the news that sex trade traffickers were preying on child survivors of Myanmar's devastating Cyclone Nargis.

The Lure of Porn

Why is pornography such a highly successful temptation? The simple yet true answer is evil desire in the heart. Evil intentions in the heart, which have existed since the fall of mankind, are what motivate all sinful behavior. God's fierce wrath was provoked in Noah's day because the evil "intention of the thoughts of [man's] heart was only evil continually" (Genesis 6:5). The ability to depict pornographic images with art or photography is not the root problem: it's evil in the heart.

Our modern society is influenced by the same motives and intentions of the heart. Pornography has always been more than an enticing image. From drawing with a piece of charcoal, to painting with bright colors, to taking pictures of seductive women, to computer generated sexual images, the internal dynamic is the same: Each new technological development is rooted in a two-way process of interaction between the exhibitor and the viewer. Evil desire drives both of them. However, they both exist independently in their own internal wickedness. Without the viewer, the exhibitor is left alone in his evil thoughts. Without the exhibitor, the viewer is left with his vivid imagination.

The development of photography began in the sixteenth century, but the quality was poor. By the seventeenth century, printed pornography from Amsterdam was being smuggled into other European countries. In 1839, a new photographic process improved the quality of photography—and pornography. But a more dramatic change came with the invention of halftone photographic printing at the beginning of the twentieth century. This development made mass production possible and was eventually used for the production of pornographic magazines.

Technology advanced rapidly, and another dramatic shift came with the invention of the motion picture. Pornographic films were produced by the hundreds and distributed by an essentially underground distribution system. The next huge change came in the early 1980s when videotape machines became available on a large scale. Instead of hundreds of pornographic films being made each year, now thousands were produced. Anyone who wanted to watch pornography could order it through the mail and watch it in the privacy of their home.

On the heels of the video revolution came the Internet, which quickly became the preferred source of pornography. Now porn could be viewed and purchased with little potential embarrassment—twenty-four hours a day. And the development of live chats made anonymous interaction with other people very easy.

The most recent development, made possible with the affordable availability of both video and still digital cameras, is the ability of "amateurs" to make and distribute their own porn. In fact, much of the pornography available today is produced by amateurs. The digital media allows amateur porn makers to capture images in electronic files. Once these images are created, file-sharing programs allow pornographic images to be easily and widely exchanged. Pornography, rather than music, is the most frequent use of such programs. According to an analysis[14] of over twenty-two million searches on file-sharing networks, one study found the following:

- 73 percent of all movie searches were for pornography
- 24 percent of all image searches were for child pornography
- 6 percent of all searches were for child pornography of some kind

- Only 3 percent were for non-pornographic or non-copyrighted materials

Yet, technology is not the real enemy at the center of the problem. The evil in the heart takes a neutral medium and makes it serve an evil purpose. The misuse of technology consistently gives more people what the evil intentions of their hearts have always wanted.

The Sexual Revolution

Another explanation of the sexual darkness that envelops us is the "sexual revolution." This revolution involved many events and factors in the 1960s and '70s but, historically, the origins are traced back to Alfred Kinsey's "Kinsey Report" in the 1940s and 1950s with its details of the sex lives of supposedly typical Americans. Some consider him a liberator while others see him in his personal life as a pervert.

Another factor in the sexual revolution was the publication by Hugh Hefner of the first edition of *Playboy Magazine* in 1953.

A huge contributor to the sexual revolution came in 1960 when the birth control pill freed women to have sex whenever and with whomever they wanted. Many in the feminist movement welcomed sexual freedom as an important expansion of women's rights.

Further developments in the revolution were the blending of anti-establishment and anti-war ideas that resulted in popular slogans like "make love, not war" and "do your own thing." Some women started burning bras and a pornographic movie, *Deep Throat*, was distributed in mainline theaters. Soon there were sex and hipster clubs for swingers.

The sexual revolution changed sexuality into a celebration of sexual love as an end in itself and available to anyone, single or married. Coupled with the cult of self-fulfillment and complete personal autonomy, the result is that divorce increases and more young adults live together outside of marriage.

When sexual relationships go outside the standard of one man with one woman, and one woman with one man, sexually transmitted disease will logically increase. The sexual revolution continues to this day with the efforts of gays, lesbians, and transgendered to redefine traditional norms of sexuality.

The evil desire for illicit sex permeates even what appear to be innocent media, such as the ubiquitous Craigslist. Started as a hobby by Craig

Newmark in 1995, Craigslist has local classifieds and forums in 450 cities worldwide. As I write this, just under seventeen million people visit Craigslist per month. Many of us have bought or sold an item or looked for a job or service on Craigslist. As it turns out, many visitors are looking for something other than a couch, car, or job. In eight major cities it's reported that erotic services show the highest number of individual visitors—almost twice as many as the next ranking category. In early 2007, the average was 265,000 people per city seeking illicit sex, which is over two million per month in just those eight cities![15]

The search for sex online is not that shocking when you understand that the "intentions of man's heart is evil from his youth" (Genesis 8:21). Online shopping for sex offers anonymity, and little concern for being naked and ashamed as you live out your fantasy in the privacy of your own home.

In the old days if you wanted some impersonal sex, you at least had to drive to a certain part of town or go to a bar and hope to be picked up. Now no one has to leave home and you can feed your lust every night if you want! Our situation is desperate as sexual standards continue to change at a rapid speed and godlessness spreads. In unison, humanity in one loud, rebellious temper tantrum seems to scream, "Satisfy my lust now!" And as has always been the case, greed and technology rise to the occasion.

British anthropologist J. D. Unwin studied eighty-six cultures spanning five thousand years of human history and found that, without exception, cultures thrive when they restrict sex to marriage. He also found that no culture survived more than three generations after disregarding that standard.[16]

Where does that leave our society? While it would be foolish to ignore the threat, I don't think this is the place or time to surrender by declaring that our society is on the verge of collapse. For there to be sexual redemption, we must first acknowledge that a serious problem exists and then identify its true nature.

It would be bad enough if this sexual darkness were only evident in the broader culture. Perhaps we shouldn't be surprised by the extent to which Christians are also trapped in the same muck—the topic of the next chapter.

The Path to Sexual Redemption

1 What evidence of "sexual darkness" do you observe in others? Being honest, in yourself?

2 Have you ever considered that the "evil intentions of the heart" are the root cause of sexual immorality?

3 Jesus said, "What comes out of a person is what defiles him. For from within, out of the heart of man, come evil thoughts, sexual immorality, theft, murder, adultery, coveting, wickedness, deceit, sensuality, envy, slander, pride, foolishness. All these evil things come from within, and they defile a person" (Mark 7:20–23). Ask God to reveal areas in your own internal disposition that are defiling you.

CHAPTER THREE

The Struggle for Christians

My lips are ready to confess,
But my heart is slow to feel,
And my ways reluctant to amend.
I bring my soul to thee;
Break it, wound it, bend it, mold it.
Unmask to me sin's deformity,
That I may hate it, abhor it, flee from it.[1]

In the same phone call with Jim (see the beginning of chapter 2), I offered him encouragement. I told him to hold steady and explained to him that in spite of the pain and desperate circumstances, God was at work.

The first revelation of unfaithfulness is a violent betrayal of the marriage vows that tears the fragile ties of any marriage bond to shreds. When more sexual sin is uncovered later, after a spouse believes they have been told everything, the damage is five times more destructive.

"Jim, I need to talk with Carrie, will she talk with me?" I asked him. He went on to explain that Carrie had kicked him out of the house—for the second time—and now he was living with his brother.

"I don't know if she will talk or not, but please call her," he said. "She started seeing a counselor here in town and the guy told her she has biblical grounds for divorce. I know you have an intensive counseling session scheduled for next week. Please, can you somehow fit us in?"

In fact, we had just had a rare cancellation. "If Carrie is willing to come, you two can take that opening," I said.

"Please call her," Jim said. "Carrie will not talk to me or return my calls. I'll check on airline flights and wait to hear from you."

During my first conversation with Carrie, in complete confusion and disbelief she had said about Jim, "I just don't get it! He's a good father and we're leaders in our church. I feel like I don't know who this man is anymore!"

At first glance it is hard to comprehend how men and women who clearly know the truth fall so easily into sexual temptation and sin. "What are they thinking?" is another common question I hear. Actually, as we gain a deeper understanding of the issues, we are not so surprised. And we should not be proud and too quick to point an accusing finger. As I will show, we all need sexual redemption.

But what really is going on with Christians? In counseling almost fifteen hundred Christian couples from all age groups, various educational and economic backgrounds, and from all geographic areas of the United States, I've found that among that group over 85 percent were sexually intimate before marriage. All have had some type of heart or physical unfaithfulness in their marriage, and about 85 percent were also sexually dissatisfied or dysfunctional. In most cases the wife had little or no sexual interest. Some husbands were struggling with relationally specific erectile dysfunction.

Various studies, as well as more informal data, indicate that about half of Christians are dealing with some level of involvement with Internet pornography. The following is a portion of an open letter to the church that author and pastor Chuck Swindoll published on his Insight for Living website:

> The most recent studies available suggest that 1 out of every 2 people—that's 50% of the people sitting in our pews—are looking at and/or could be addicted to Internet pornography. The struggle is going on among those who volunteer in your church and mine. Chances are good that some of our

full-time staff members, even some who faithfully serve on our boards, may be losing this secret battle. And while I'm listing these possibilities, let's not overlook our young adults—married and single—who provide instruction among our junior and senior high youth. Truth be told, that statistic could be even higher.[2]

It's difficult for many of us to believe that up to 50 percent of our fellow attendees on a Sunday morning are looking at porn on the Internet. One pastor was skeptical, so he surveyed his own congregation. He found that 60 percent had looked at pornography within the past year, and 25 percent within the past thirty days.[3]

Anecdotal indicators also support a disturbing problem within the church. One mission organization personally told me that 80 percent of their applicants voluntarily indicated a problem with pornography. Another interdenominational organization that trains young pastors stated that they had yet to interview a candidate who didn't have a pornography problem. Maybe even more scary is the revelation that none of their wives knew of their struggle.

An interdenominational seminary professor stated to me, "We no longer ask if an entering student struggles with pornography; we assume he does. We now ask the question: 'How serious is the problem?'"

If this plague of lust is not dealt with, the work of God will be impacted for generations to come. What will happen when young pastors, who are planting churches and starting families, suddenly have their wives discover their pornography problem? Or what happens as more and more youth pastors, full of lustful thoughts and living on the edge of ruin, influence children negatively in subtle or overt ways? Some of these leaders will fall, creating more disappointment and disillusionment in the next generation. This rot in the church must be addressed or the devastation will be incalculable.

Indicators of the Problem

Statistics and anecdotes alone do not reveal the full scope of our sexual dilemma. After counseling for thirty years, the last eighteen years devoted exclusively to sexual issues, and based on continual study of the Bible, I have observed an inherent darkness in our sexuality that certain ideas and behaviors reveal. I would like to briefly explain these subtle and not so subtle "indicators," because without some insight into where we are with our sexuality and why, it will be less clear why our need for sexual redemption is so urgent.

I want to review this evidence in some detail because there is a temptation to think that sexual abnormalities are limited to "addicts" or people manifesting extreme behavior. That's not true. I don't want to let anyone off the hook who might say, "That's not my problem."

Indicator 1: Diminished Femininity and Masculinity

With just about every man and woman I have counseled, single or married, I have encountered what I describe as diminished masculinity and femininity. For men, this manifests itself as a lack of leadership, male bashing, spiritual emptiness, and the dynamic of male passivity that can be described pointedly as "men are wimps." In women I observe a lack of sexual interest and a hardness that avoids "a gentle and quiet spirit" (see 1 Peter 3:4) so as not to feel weak, but this will always result in a less than truly attractive woman. Yes, outwardly she looks attractive, but pay careful attention to her face, her tone of voice, and her attitude and you begin to see a loss of genuine strength and beauty. Along with it comes increasing bitterness, a desire to be in control, and a spirituality-lite where women avoid the spiritually empty man and turn to find "Jesus as their lover." The pointed description of women, similar to the "men are wimps" refrain, is "women are witches." One of the signs of diminished femininity and masculinity is that the wife feels like a mother with her husband, and the husband feels like a child with his wife.

I believe that relationally specific impotence in men and a lack of sexual desire in women (see Indicator 2) relate to diminished masculinity and femininity: If you feel like a child around your wife, wouldn't impotence be a problem? When a man has an affair, he often struggles less than he does with his wife and fools himself into feeling more like a man. Likewise for a woman, if you feel like a mother around your husband, wouldn't there be a lack of sexual desire? When a woman has an affair she is looking for a fulfilling relationship, and sexual desire is never the problem. Diminished masculinity and femininity are internal heart issues and point directly to the need for sexual redemption.

Indicator 2: Sexual Dysfunction

I frequently run into this issue with couples I counsel. The common female symptom is loss of sexual desire; for males, it is impotence. I don't think you can catch the evening news on any of the major networks or watch a televised sporting event without seeing an ad for a pill that promises to fix the "male problem." The drug Viagra was developed by Pfizer and approved by the FDA in 1998. It was an immediate hit with $1 billion in sales between 1999 and 2001. The obvious conclusion: men have a problem. But before yelling "viva Viagra" and asking your doctor for a prescription, let's take a closer look at what's going on in the male sexual soul.

Of course, there are physical factors that can cause impotence that need to be ruled out by a physician. For example, almost 60 percent of adult-onset diabetes cases in men are first detected via the symptom of impotence. However, in my counseling experience, impotency—unless it's a medical problem—is often relationally specific. By that I mean that a married man who cannot have an erection with his wife may often have no problem doing so while masturbating or in intercourse with another woman. Why is this?

It is foolhardy to overlook the relational (and I believe ultimately spiritual) context of sexuality. The medical model assumes we can solve genital and other physical difficulties without regard to relational or spiritual factors. A pill may help fix the sexual part that isn't working, but it can do little or nothing to change deep relational or spiritual problems.

With the woman, sexual dysfunction is revealed when she has no apparent desire for intimacy or to please her partner. Or in some cases the woman's sexual dysfunction is expressed through her hiding her true feelings because she does not want to offend, lose, or anger a partner. I think it's only a matter of time before Viagra-type drugs will be available and aggressively marketed to women to solve their sexual dissatisfactions/dysfunctions, but again ignoring the deeper relational and spiritual elements.

Indicator 3: Impersonal Married Sex

What is going on behind closed doors in the marriage bed? Between 1991 and 2008 in our intensive counseling workshop, we worked with over three thousand Christians from every state and eighteen foreign countries. Half of those who came were struggling with pornography issues, and of this group (mainly couples) over 90 percent of the wives—even before the pornography was discovered—would identify with the fear and distrust expressed by one wife who confessed: "Whenever my husband and I make love, I wonder what he is thinking. I don't trust how he touches me. It doesn't feel like love. I feel like a sexual object."

I believe that impersonal sex is common in many Christian marriages. To be very blunt, these couples are no longer truly intimate but are engaging in vaginal masturbation. To top it off, some Christian sex therapists have encouraged couples to use pornography to solve their intimacy problems. Let's say that an imaginary couple, Ted and Linda, follow this advice. Ted becomes sexually aroused by the women in a pornographic video instead of Linda. Linda imagines having sex with the man in the video rather than Ted. When they do have sex, the important question to ask is, who are they really having sex with? They are touching each other physically, but are they making love with each other? Not if their focus and attention are on some other person. Obviously, getting "my needs met" is not the supreme goal of marriage. Bringing glory to God is. Sex without true intimacy is dishonoring to God, because He designed human marital intimacy to be a representation of divine intimacy.

Behind all impersonal sex in marriage I have found the existence of diminished femininity and masculinity (as described above), self-centeredness, fear of rejection on the part of men, and fear of vulnerability on the part of women. Another significant factor is styles of relating that attempt to control the sexual/relational experience.

Indicator 4: The Beauty Myth

For men and women, "beauty" has become nearly synonymous with "sexy." The beauty myth, an obsession with physical perfection, holds women in bondage to hopelessness, self-consciousness, and self-hatred. It intertwines sexuality and beauty to create the idea that a woman must be "beautiful" to be sexual and desirable in a relationship. Women say they "feel sexier" when they lose weight, but female sexual pleasure doesn't multiply with weight loss. Compared with sexual sin, the obsession with beauty may seem like a minor issue. In reality, however, the impossible-to-achieve desire to secure an external "flawless beauty" destroys a woman's sexuality and spirituality.

The "pornography of beauty" reshapes female sexuality. You see this in everyday magazine ads and in women's magazines. Users of Photoshop have taken the picture of a three hundred pound woman in lingerie and turned her into a sex goddess. There is little that is real about such an image, but men and women will worship it. The image-altering software easily creates the perfect hair, skin, and figure. The message is clear: "Look like that if you want to feel like *that*."

Why does a woman go under the knife for numerous facelifts in a desperate attempt to look younger? Why are girls much more self-conscious about their appearance today? Why did my mother, in her early nineties, still dye her hair? The beauty myth has obscured what is truly beautiful in a woman. I can still vaguely remember when being a woman meant something more than dress size. Today we are easily duped into thinking that external beauty is all there is to a woman.

More and more women believe they must have *that* face and look to have their needs met. Like sexual pornography, the pornography of beauty is based on a myth and both types of porn make a woman an object. If a man's image and understanding of sexuality is distorted by pornography, I suggest that there is a parallel effect on a woman's image and her understanding of sexuality in the beauty myth.

Unfortunately, the beauty myth is winning the battle against sexual purity. In reality the ads don't sell sex; instead they sell discontent, shame, and guilt. A woman will say, "I hate my body, my hips, my thighs, and my stomach." This is at the core a deep sexual shame, which is destructive both relationally and spiritually. And this focus on external beauty is in direct contradiction to what Scripture teaches—that authentic beauty comes from inside a person:

> Do not let your adorning be external—the braiding of hair and the putting on of gold jewelry, or the clothing you wear—but let your adorning be the hidden person of the heart with the imperishable beauty of a gentle and quiet spirit, which in God's sight is very precious. For this is how the holy women who hoped in God used to adorn themselves, by submitting to their own husbands, as Sarah obeyed Abraham, calling him lord. And you are her children, if you do good and do not fear anything that is frightening. (1 Peter 3:3–6)

Indicator 5: Lustful Intent

Lust is a huge problem. Outside the church, men routinely comment among themselves about the shape, form, and size of women walking by. Inside the church such crude comments are unacceptable so men just look and keep their thoughts to themselves. No one but God knows the spiritual harm and destructiveness that goes on around us. "Men are visual!" states the obvious, but should we accept lustful intent as normal for men?

Everyone believes that every man struggles with lust, but even if true, that certainly doesn't make it right; sin is also the norm, but it still remains sin. In one of Jesus' strongest exhortations, He unequivocally condemns lust: "Everyone who looks at a woman with lustful intent has already committed adultery with her in his heart" (Matthew 5:28). Jesus' demand to "tear out" whatever causes one to sin (Matthew 5:29–30) has nothing to do with self-mutilation because the problem doesn't originate in the eye or the hand, but the heart, then the mind. The failure to avoid lustful intent, that is, looking at a woman for the purpose of lusting *for* her, is a failure to maintain exclusive devotion to your wife (or future wife), to operate at a level of unbelief, a disregard for God and women, and to miss the point of Christian living where we treat all women "in all purity" (1 Timothy 5:2).[4]

Godly men will certainly notice modesty and appreciate it. In fact, even unbelievers can be greatly impacted by a woman's appearance that is exhibited from the inside out, according to Peter (1 Peter 3:1–4). Lust begins in the heart, not in the mind. The heart is the center of a person's identity and will. Jesus is telling us that it is not enough to maintain physical purity—mental purity and faithfulness are required too. In spiritual and sexual leadership, we men must own this problem, help one another, and protect our wives, sisters, and daughters from being sexual objects. To do that, we must start in our own hearts. We will explore this further in later chapters.

Indicator 6: Declining Modesty

Immodesty parallels the problem with lust. Both are heart issues, both mar the image of God, both are spiritually and relationally destructive. When all is said and done, a godly husband must keep his focus on what is precious to him and guard it for himself. A godly wife must keep her focus on what is precious to her husband and guard it for him alone.

One missionary, the wife of an executive, complained to me about the low necklines of women in the mission's headquarters and her husband's daily exposure to these women. How different are Christian women from non-Christians in the area of modesty? Have we become a church that has lost its respect for female modesty? Have we adapted to the culture around us to the point that modesty is associated with sexual repression? How a woman dresses is more than a fashion statement. A wife whose husband had committed adultery said to me, "Wearing a halter top with a very sexy bra and short, tight shorts is a combination created to draw attention. I like to look hot when I go out. I like to be looked at. Looking hot gives me a sense of power over men. It boosts my confidence and helps me feel good about myself."

How a woman—and for that matter a man—dresses and grooms herself reflects on how seriously she takes scriptural admonition and it reveals the motivation of her heart.

God created women in His image, which allows them to develop an eye for creative beauty both in themselves and their surroundings. Dressing provocatively may seem like a fashion statement, but Peter warns against a preoccupation with outward appearance. Godly women focus on inward beauty, what is in the heart (see 1 Peter 3:1–6). I believe many women are unaware of the dangers and spiritual destruction of wanting to be accepted and admired for what they wear. They go day to day enjoying the looks, the attention, and the feelings that are stimulated by outward appearance. Some will think that I'm "legalistic" and certainly "out of style," but I write as a concerned man for the women around me and I know how men distort created beauty for their own purpose. Given this reality, and in light of Paul's exhortation for "modesty and self-control" (1 Timothy 2:9–10), we should be careful not to reinterpret God's Word to our liking. Men, as husbands and fathers, along with the women they love, must take full responsibility for the manner of dress. However, it is not about clothes, it's about the heart. The good heart will avoid anything that is overly revealing or sexually appealing. Each woman must examine her motives and goals for how she dresses. A woman may want to flaunt her appearance or even look sexy to men. Men don't think about the difference; either way, the message is "look at me." Both goals distract attention from true beauty. What makes a woman attractive is what points to God and His glory. This should be the preoccupation of every woman who desires her life to be characterized by "good works," "imperishable beauty," and a "pure heart."

Indicator 7: Premarital Sex

Premarital sex among Christians is widespread. Of all the Christian couples I've counseled, I estimate that less than 20 percent were virgins when they married. Remaining a virgin until marriage, a practice all but lost within the church, is still God's standard, but I have not found in my counseling practice that sexual dysfunction correlates with the premartial sexual experience. I have never met a married couple struggling with a lack of desire or impotence that had the same problems in their premarital sexual experience. Why is this? As we will see as I further develop our understanding of sexual redemption, I believe the drastic changes and sexual dissatisfaction/dysfunction that take place after marriage are directly related to relational and spiritual problems.

Indicator 8: The Acceptance of Masturbation

We cannot ignore the issue of masturbation. Respected Christian authorities are divided over whether masturbation is a sin or a valid sexual expression for singles or spouses with sexual dissatisfaction. In addition, the difficulty of addressing the issue is compounded by the reluctance to talk about it. Scripture is silent on the subject, though some have equated Onan's act (Genesis 38:8–10) with masturbation and one term for masturbation is *onanism*. However, his behavior did not involve manual stimulation but coitus interruptus.

Christian supporters of masturbation argue the following points:

- It enables us to enjoy our bodies and God's gift of sexual pleasure
- It's an alternative to premarital sex
- It's an alternative to sinful behavior such as adultery
- It provides gratification for men and women who are sexually dissatisfied in marriage
- It allows us to reap the health benefits of sexual release
- It prevents sexually transmitted diseases
- It prevents unwanted pregnancies

A major assumption in this line of reasoning is the centrality of personal well-being and personal needs. With that assumption, masturbation can be justified and encouraged. However, I believe that satisfaction in God and loving others will take us in a different direction.[5]

Indicator 9: Hooking Up

"Hooking up" is another indicator of what we are doing to ourselves and to others through impersonal sex. The practice was already well established by about the year 2000 when almost every American child over the age of nine knew that hooking up had something to do with sexual activity. Most parents were still in the dark, thinking the term meant "meeting" someone.

"Hooking up" is another manifestation of the mind-set that "If it harms no one, do what you want." How times have changed. During my teen years getting to "first base" referred to embracing and kissing. "Second base" meant groping, fondling, and deep or "French" kissing or "heavy petting." "Third base" referred to fellatio or "oral sex." "Home plate" meant intercourse or "going all the way."

In today's world the sexual particulars of hooking up vary but generally speaking "first base" means deep kissing ("tonsil hockey"), groping, and fondling; "second base" means "oral sex;" "third base" means sexual intercourse; and "home plate" means learning the other person's name. That's not a joke: For many teenagers and young adults, dating is seen as a drain on their energy and intellectual resources. Fully intimate, interpersonal relationships are not highly valued.

Among college students, 70 percent have participated in at least one hookup (75 percent of men, 84 percent of women). Of those who have hooked up, 91 percent report doing it more than once. The average number of hookups for both men and women is 10.28 during their college career. Students report that 55 percent of their hookups involved anonymous partners; 49 percent report that hookups are planned in terms of occurrence but not in the choice of a partner. According to the survey, 69 percent of hookup partners do not communicate during their sexual encounter, while 25 percent engage in small talk.[6]

In the not-too-distant past a one-night stand and uncommitted sex had to be justified, whereas for many people having sex in a committed relationship was okay. Now the random, uncommitted sexual encounter seems the norm among many high school and college students. But hooking up is a false intimacy, an obstacle to real intimacy that will define a whole generation's character and way of life. By viewing sex as a means to an end rather than the expression of a relationship, millions are rendering themselves incapable of a meaningful relationship in the future.

Impersonal sex is also medically dangerous. The more sexual encounters one has, the more chance there is of being infected with a sexually transmitted disease (STD). The STD rate is higher in the United States than any other developed country. There was a time when parents were concerned that a daughter would lose her virginity and become pregnant. Added to those worries now is the fear of Chlamydia, which, if not treated, can lead to infertility.

A condom can protect against pregnancy, but there is no device to protect a girl or boy from the relational and spiritual destruction of hooking up.

Today's young adults are fooling themselves when they engage in false intimacy, distancing sexual intimacy from relational intimacy. The girl who sleeps with a guy she doesn't know feels like an object. It's impossible for a human being, made in the image of God and created for meaningful relationship, to master attachment-free hooking up. Those who hook up have to deny the natural feelings of connection that are an inseparable part of sex and work hard—even harder than they are willing to admit—to deny that something is dying on the inside.

Studies show that among women who hook up, the predominant feeling is regret, centered around shame and self-blame—all compounded by the pain of not knowing their partner and the unlikelihood of further contact. Men feel regret centered around how unattractive their choice was in a partner.[7]

Is the situation much different on the Christian college campus? While writing this book in 2008, a family member visiting his daughter at a small midwest rural Bible college found the doors locked on a beautiful campus chapel. When he asked why, he was told this was to prevent students from having sex in the building. Women on this campus described the same type of impersonal sex found at non-Christian schools, only with a different term: "make-out buddies." It's just hooking up with a different name. The students are not dating and don't greet each other when they pass in the halls. Does this not make you want to weep?

I am not implying that the situation is as bad on Christian college campuses, and certainly these schools are not endorsing such activity. Donna Freitas, author of *Sex & the Soul: Juggling Sexuality, Spirituality, Romance, and Religion on America's College Campuses*, crisscrossed the country interviewing students at seven colleges and universities. She visited Catholic, evangelical, nonreligious, private, and public schools. Freitas writes:

> Many college students seem to encounter religion and sex as if they are two powerful gods. When they interact, as they do among evangelicals, it is a battle to the death. Either religion wins, and sex withers away (until marriage, theoretically), or sex wins and faith flounders. . . . For the most part, students at evangelical and spiritual colleges have strikingly different college experiences. But their experiences are alike in four ways: 1) They are highly invested in their religious and/or spiritual identities. 2) They experience sexual desire and long to act on that desire. 3) Romance and experiencing

a fulfilling romantic relationship are priorities. 4) They don't know how to reconcile 1–3.[8]

This book by Donna Freitas may provide some comfort that evangelical colleges are different from all other schools. But we must not be lulled into a false sense of security, only to wake up too late to a dramatic shift on the Christian campus. Perhaps we are still in a time when Christian kids hold less sexually permissive attitudes than other youth. But I believe they are not the last ones to engage in sexual immorality, on average. Tragically, we strongly encourage our kids to dedicate themselves to living the Christian life and to the high priorities of family and sexual purity, but as Mark Regnerus states in *Forbidden Fruit*, "Evangelical youth, if their affiliation is not combined with active religious involvement and practice, are not simply identical to the rest of the world when it comes to sexual experience during adolescence, they are actually more active."[9]

The trend toward more impersonal sex is reflected in a teenage young man from a strong Christian home with high standards of sexual purity who said to me: "I don't have a girlfriend, but I meet with several girls and we get physically involved. I justify my sinful actions by telling myself it's better than looking at porn and masturbating." We have high school teens putting off dating until college and just being friends, but now it's "friends with benefits."

This is really just a brief review of the symptoms and indicators of the sexual darkness around and within us. But what really is at the core of the problem with our spirituality and sexuality?

Some would say that to a large degree those who struggle to overcome sexual temptations are unable to do so because of basic sexual hardwiring of the brain or an addiction that is tied to an incurable disease. Let's take a look at those ideas next.

The Path to Sexual Redemption

1 Whether you are single or married, what problems have you struggled with sexually? Premarital sex, masturbation, hooking up?

2 If you are a man, do you experience spiritual emptiness, feel like a child around your wife, or find yourself wimping out?

3 If you are a woman, is there a hardness distorting your true femininity?

4 In all honesty, have you been reluctant to unmask your spiritual and sexual struggles?

CHAPTER FOUR

Is This a Disease?

O my crucified but never wholly mortified sinfulness!
O my life-long damage and daily shame!
O my indwelling and besetting sins!
O the tormenting slavery of a sinful heart!
Destroy, O God, the dark guest within
whose hidden presence makes my life a hell.[1]

After hearing Jim's desperation about the possible loss of his marriage, I immediately called his estranged wife, Carrie. Another woman answered—I learned this was Carrie and Jim's married daughter, Susan. I explained who I was and Carrie got on the line.

"Do you know what this man did?" she asked defensively. "I don't know who this man is; I can't stay in this marriage; I wouldn't stay in this marriage! I don't believe God would want me to."

We talked for some time about the details of what Jim had done online with other women and how she was hurting.

"Is there any hope for somebody like him?" Carrie asked angrily. "Or is he just a sex addict who will always be like he is? I think he's sick! Why else would he treat me this way—and hurt our whole family?" She started to cry.

I attempted to answer her questions, explaining that I did not think Jim was incurable or could not change. He would have to face the reality that he was trapped in serious sin. But the cross provides an answer to sin. As we talked, Carrie softened, then said, "I know I'm crazy, but I still love him. My counselor is telling me to divorce, and my friends says it's the right thing to do. But deep inside I want to do what God wants. But I just can't imagine living like *this*."

How I respond to a hurting person like Carrie is a reflection of my personal experience with the Word of God. Scripture reveals that pain is unavoidable in our broken world; but, more importantly, I also find in the Word—even though sorrow is penetratingly deep—a God who is at work. Like Joseph's brothers, what an unfaithful spouse meant as evil, God meant for good (Genesis 50:20). I feel my own pain, and I feel someone else's pain. In it all there is an Ultimate Reality greater than our painful situations. At *all* times we are to pursue the path that glorifies God.

As I have already indicated, based on my study of Scripture, as well as my training and years of experience as a counselor, I believe the root cause of sexual immorality is simply and plainly sin. And the way to overcome such sin is through sexual redemption. You may be thinking, *Well, of course it's sin! Looking at porn or having an affair is sin—everybody knows that!* I suppose most people, particularly Christians, would know that, but how to describe and deal with such sin—even in Christian circles—causes significant disagreement. I think it wise to at least briefly discuss the major ideas about what is going on with people who are struggling sexually and what the potential solutions are.

It's All in Your Head?

You may not be aware of it, but extensive scientific study in recent years has been devoted to monogamy in prairie voles! Why? Because scientists believe it's possible that what goes on in their genes, brains, and nests resembles what goes on in the genes, brains, and bedrooms of human beings. As absurd as this may sound, it makes some sense if God is not the originator and designer of human sexuality.

The theory under review is that the feel-good chemical dopamine that is important to voles plays an important role in human society; for example, in love, social attachment, and reward. Thus researchers believe that there are great similarities between our sexuality and relational patterns and those of voles. Studies show that voles can associate a particular partner with reward. So the conclusion is that romantic love, our "reward," has now become an addiction, just a chemical reaction.

This is how it works: A man meets a woman on Saturday night. During a pleasing conversation, the man feels some "chemistry" and starts to fall in love. The two have several dates and exchange long embraces and kisses. The man says to the woman, "I want you. I can't live without you." This is like an addiction to cocaine, where the user has a certain dose and then needs more to get the same thrill. Unfortunately, in this scenario, the woman pulls back and won't see the guy anymore. He feels pain and goes into a withdrawal—crying, depression, the whole bit.

Several months pass and the man and woman encounter each other at church. She smiles and touches his shoulder affectionately. He senses a change in her attitude and asks, "Do you want to have lunch?" She gives that certain smile and says yes. His body tingles. This is a relapse of his "addiction" because once again he has the good feelings of romantic love. What's the difference between this man and a vole? The man has a larger brain and lives under greater pressure than a vole.

If you are over forty and reading this, you may find this discussion ridiculous. Don't laugh too hard too quickly. Apparently, many Christian counselors make use of such research in some aspects of their therapy with clients. As an example, in the area of sexual sin, it's believed that the "addict's" brain doesn't discern his sexual behavior as moral or immoral. It's a brain chemical issue. A brain-imaging specialist wrote in a leading Christian counseling magazine:

> Your brain decides who is attractive to you, how to get a date, how well you do on the date, what to do with the feelings that develop, how long those feelings last, when to commit, and how well you do as a partner and a parent. When your brain works right, it helps you to be thoughtful, playful, romantic, intimate, committed, and loving with your partner. When the brain is dysfunctional, it causes you to be impulsive, distracted, addicted, unfaithful, angry, and even hateful, thus ruining the chances for continued intimacy and love.[2]

I ask, What happened to human choice, will, and the deceitful heart?

Author Os Guinness has predicted that the way of interpreting life after postmodernism will be guided by the belief that everything can be understood as chemical.[3] I think his prediction is already coming true, at least in the counseling world. I don't deny that everything about the functioning of my body involves chemicals, but is that it? Can being made in God's image and likeness be reduced to chemical reactions?

Absolutely not!

The Therapeutic Revolution

The solutions to suffering in relationships are varied and never ending. Combine the need to be cherished and the disappointment of not being cherished with today's entrepreneurial spirit, and you have what is called the "therapeutic revolution." Much of counseling focuses on a person's ability to cope with negative feelings and conform behavior to a more functional standard. Counseling may have an important role, but only if it goes beyond the symptoms to the real human problem on the inside.

Many find counseling beneficial, but for others their lives remain unchanged. It is even possible to be harmed by the process. Counseling often focuses on the past and creates, along with our therapeutic culture, a view of being a victim of childhood events. Such a view may lead to increased self-pity and contradicts the gospel through the belief that life is determined by past events and is therefore unchangeable. Serious spiritual impact comes from increased anger, self-pity, and bitterness over what has been done to us. Are we being held captive by a therapeutic culture and without even knowing it?

Dr. Paul Vitz was Professor of Psychology at New York University for thirty-nine years. His works are focused on the integration of Christian theology and psychology, breaking from the secular humanism and postmodern relativism prevalent today. He divides modern psychology into three parts. First, the psychology of "self-esteem," found in books, sermons, seminars, and the classroom. Second, the experience of individual counseling that has been used by millions of Americans. And third, what he calls "group psychotherapy," best seen in the recovery group movement.

Dr. Vitz states that "research shows that measures of self-esteem have no reliable relationship to behavior, either positive or negative. In part, this is simply because life is too complicated for so simple a notion."[4]

In a minority voice Dr. Vitz challenges the modern recovery movement and I suspect offends many in the process. "There is now good evidence that the disease theory of alcoholism is a mistake. An addiction is very serious and destructive, but it does not appear to be a disease."[5]

Consequences of the Disease Approach

Why is the disease model so entrenched? This is a question author Ed Welch asks. "It is not the claims of science that persuade people that addictions are best understood as a disease." Rather, Welch suggests that "the disease theory persists because there are so few readily available explanations for why people feel out of control."[6]

I think he is correct, but I'll take it a step further. The disease theory of sexual addiction persists in popularity because without a biblical understanding of sin and how to biblically gain self-control, many assume that there is no other offer of help than the disease theory. In addition, many have tried what they believe to be a Christian approach to dealing with sin and have experienced repeated failure, so they turn to what appears to be a viable alternative. And finally, in our deceitful hearts, I believe we would rather have a disease than have something really wrong with us that is evil.

This book in its entirety provides that neglected biblical explanation and offers living hope through sexual redemption.

If sin is reduced to psychosis or to a disease, then the sexual addict is not only powerless over his or her addiction, but hope is reduced to a level of progress in controlling behavior, a pride in sobriety, and a relationship with God for therapeutic well-being rather than a complete dependence on Him, His grace, and His power.

Are We Sick or Sinning?

The evangelical church has been forced into an unwilling awareness that there is sexual sin in our midst. Greater awareness of the problem has stimulated new ministries, books, and techniques. In desperation for help we can fall prey to a psychological diagnosis and to labeling a serious problem a new biological disease. The disease concept weakens an already frayed understanding of sin within the church as we entertain the inadvisable idea that "using the words *addiction* and *disease* gives clarity and deeper meaning to the word *sin*."[7] In truth, the gospel is most powerful in changing us when we know and believe in our hearts that sin *is* sin.

With open minds we must realize how easy it is for well-meaning people to be misled by wrong ideas, or as the apostle Paul put it, deluded by "plausible arguments" (Colossians 2:4). It is time to draw a line in our minds that clearly defines the truth, a truth we not only believe but use to guide our hearts and lives. We can't afford, in this postmodern era, to say we believe in sin and then turn away from the power of the gospel to use human techniques to heal a deceitful heart. Snapping a rubber band on your wrist, telling your secret sins in a group to find acceptance and comfort, or daily checking in with a sponsor will never conquer the sin that "clings so closely" (Hebrews 12:1).

I will likely be accused of being unscientific, but we cannot afford to remove in the slightest way human responsibility by theorizing that natural brain chemicals, androgens, or changes in neural circuits are the cause of compulsive sexual behavior. Physical and familial factors may exist, but without conviction and the application of grace the best we can hope to achieve is frustrating, long-term behavioral management versus authentic and lasting heart change. Sexual sin is not merely human failure: we have failed God, the Ultimate Reality.

We must beware of any philosophy that does not correctly recognize the sinful nature and that redemption in the cross of Christ is the only foundation for real change. Hundreds of thousands of people turn on their computers every day with all the intentions of checking their email and avoiding cybersex. If no one is looking, before they open their first email, there is a powerful urge to point and click on the forbidden. In the next moment they are sexually chatting or sexual images are filling their screen. In a second they have reconnected to their own hell. When the sexual encounter is complete, shame floods their being and they vow never to do it again. But tomorrow will be no different than today.

Scripture is relevant to this lack of control because it not only offers an explanation of this bondage of corruptness, but shows a way out. Sexual redemption is that way!

Some will accuse me of splitting hairs and overreacting, but sound teaching is critical in finding a lasting answer to sexual sin. As Paul warns us, "For the time is coming when people will not endure sound teaching, but having itching ears they will accumulate for themselves teachers to suit their own passions, and will turn away from listening to the truth and wander off into myths" (2 Timothy 4:3–4).

The idea of a disease and addiction treatment points to a different cause of our problems: that a person is a victim of others and/or their brain chemicals. The Word of God reveals that none of those things in and of themselves can force us to violate God's commands. Original corruption and the deceitfulness of our self-centered heart with all of its idolatrous passions is the driving force. It is that internal reality in all of us that compounds our sinful actions so that we shouldn't be surprised at the dire physical symptoms or consequences of sin. Self-help isn't enough; we need Christ's rescue operation to deliver us both from the judgment of God that is to come and the hellish bondage. There are actual sexual sins, but the ultimate problem is original corruption caused by Adam's primal sin (Romans 5:12–21). Both the actual sexual sins and the original corruption condemn a person before God. That is why all forms of self-improvement in this life are inadequate for the job.

Disease theory *may* offer some assistance in managing the behavior itself, but this approach does not clearly state that the great spiritual battle for delight in God is not only critical in this life but crucial for eternity. That is, to love God and be satisfied in Him is absolutely essential to glorifying God, and glorifying God is the only reason for life.

Scripture teaches that we must fight to have a true satisfaction in God alone, not just change our external behavior. Disease theory doesn't motivate us to deal with our self-centeredness and to cry out as David did after his sin with Bathsheba, "Create in me a clean heart, O God, and renew a right spirit within me" (Psalm 51:10).

One of the men I've counseled related his struggle to gain victory by following the recommendations of a self-help book and "gutting it out" with personal discipline. Of course, the principles and effort he describes are not necessarily wrong or bad. However, most of the time, approaches like these are ultimately ineffective in overcoming sin.

> I remember coming to a place where I'd had enough. I decided that I was going to win over this sexual addiction. I started reading a book on temptation and decided I would do everything that the author recommended.
>
> For nine months I was pornography free, while reading a chapter a day in this book. I read the book through four times in a row. I did everything the book said, except for one, and that was to share my struggles with a group of Christian brothers. This was something I was not willing to do, knowing that if I talked to even one individual, the "cat would be out of the bag" and my life as I knew it would be over.
>
> I struggled with my addiction in loneliness, since I would not let anyone inside. Not even my wife was a part of my private world. I felt like I was the only man involved in a Christian ministry that struggled in this fashion. I always felt, if people really knew me, they would not like me, so I let no

one in. I remember the book telling me that I would not be able to have victory over this addiction alone, but I was going to prove the book wrong and show them how discipline and hard work could make it happen.

Everything was going fine until one day I was tired, discouraged, and depressed. To solve this problem, I went back to my sexual addiction and fell hard. I was so discouraged I didn't know what to do. I needed help.

The Dark Inside

So much has changed in the long journey from a few simple sexual drawings on a scroll to the dark side of high-speed Internet access, anytime, anywhere. At the same time, nothing has changed on the inside of fallen humanity. In Colossians 3:5, Paul tells his readers to "Put to death, therefore, what is earthly in you: sexual immorality . . ." The original word in the Greek translated sexual immorality is *porneia*. Our English word *pornography* is derived from *porneia* + *graph*, or "immoral writing." *Porneia* originally referred to any excessive behavior or lack of restraint. Eventually it became associated with sexual excess and indulgence. *Porneia* used in the Scriptures describes *any* illicit sexual activity outside of the divine bounds of marriage, including, but not limited to, adultery, premarital sex, homosexuality, bestiality, incest, and prostitution.

Jesus taught clearly about humanity's dark internal disposition. "For from within, out of the heart of man, come evil thoughts, sexual immorality, theft, murder, adultery, coveting, wickedness, deceit, sensuality, envy, slander, pride, foolishness. All these evil things come from within, and they defile a person" (Mark 7:21–23). What transpires on the inside of the heart has to do with "impurity, passion, evil desire" (Colossians 3:5). Impurity describes any substance that is filthy or dirty and could refer to human refuse or the contents of graves. No wonder Jesus says it's what's on the inside that defiles a person. "For you are like whitewashed tombs, which outwardly appear beautiful, but *within* are full of dead people's bones and all uncleanness" (Matthew 23:27). The biblical word translated "passion" indicates a negative emotion aroused by some external object, such as sexual sin prompted by something impure. What's on the inside brings a disdain for God-glorifying sexual purity, so God abandons us to a spirit of licentiousness. "They were filled with all manner of unrighteousness, evil, covetousness, malice. They are full of envy, murder, strife, deceit, maliciousness. They are gossips, slanders, haters of God, insolent, haughty, boastful, invertors of evil, disobedient to parents, foolish, faithless, heartless, ruthless" (Romans 1:29–31).

Being a slave to our passions leads to being driven by our desires for wrong things. It is important to remember that when a believer plays around with sin, he or she is not immune to the *consequences of becoming a slave to it.* An evil desire is a strong desire that is a perversion of our God-given desires. The picture is clear: Like a vulture feeding on the decaying flesh of dead animals, a sexual sinner feeds on a foul-smelling dead skunk rather than a fine juicy steak.

The first four vices in Colossians 3:5 have to do with sexual sin, while the fifth summarizes the nature of sin—self-seeking or covetous. Every sexual sin is basically selfishness: the self is put before others. But the real violation is putting self before God—so Paul adds in Colossians 3:5, "which is idolatry." When we worship the cultural idols of self and well-being, God is no longer God. Our well-being is supreme, and we do not seek His kingdom but our own. So we live for self and justify all manner of sin. Immodesty, masturbation, adultery, voyeurism, pornography, and prostitution are all insatiable self-seeking.

If we major on our family of origin or past abuse as the cause of sexual immorality, we are not only challenging the teaching of Jesus but end up dwelling on *relatively* secondary causes. Horrific sexual abuse drives a person deeper into themselves, and we must always appreciate the magnitude of the trauma and the injustice that was committed, but never fail to see the horror of sin. I once counseled a fifty-year-old man who wept as he recounted his mother's method of physical punishment. Whenever he misbehaved she would spank his penis with a wooden spoon. The trauma fed his self-doubts, and he felt inadequate as a man. I believe he was a victim of sexual abuse. As a bisexual, he sought male approval through anonymous sexual encounters in public parks. As a married man and pastor, he knew his actions were sinful, but he insisted on seeking out male approval in this perverse way.

We can't manage lust simply by diverting the eyes; neither can we overcome any expression of sexual sin if we don't kill "what is earthly" inside of us (Colossians 3:5). Behavior can be managed to a degree, but real change from the inside out is essential and is always the work of God.

The Cause of Real Change

We must understand the proper cause and effect for real change. Start at the beginning and don't put the proverbial cart before the horse: Sin in our lives causes the enslavement of what is popularly called a sexual addiction. *In other words, disease or sexual addiction does not cause lust, adultery, or any form of sexual immorality.* You and I sin because we are sinners. A sexual sinner is dealing with the bondage that comes from what's inside—the sinful nature. The will is in bondage to sin. Therefore, we inevitably and naturally sin.

The concept of our bondage to sin is at the core of the gospel, and we shouldn't water it down with disease theory. The Bible must not be reduced to a self-help book where its value and acceptance as the truth comes from its effectiveness in making life work. (For example, "The Bible is true because it improved my marriage.") The work of God in our lives is not all about "healing ourselves" of the sins others have committed against us. Rather, the work of God is mainly about being healed by God of the sins *we* have committed.

Only biblical truth gives a clear and comprehensive understanding of our human nature and situation and reveals the solution for real change. The concept of sexual addiction, so popular in Christian counseling and in recovery groups, does not help us define the true nature of sexual sin.

Thankfully, the gospel remains powerful to heal and restore.

The Path to Sexual Redemption

❶ Do you agree or disagree that sexual problems like "addiction to pornography" are a disease? Explain your answer.

❷ How would you explain the meaning of the comment, "We sin because we are sinners"?

❸ In your struggle with sexual immorality, have you ever identified the cause of the problem and your lack of self-control as "what is earthly in you" (Colossians 3:5), your own internal disposition?

CHAPTER FIVE

Why Is Sex Such a Big Deal?

I do not play when I sink in deep mire,
for sin is no game, no toy, no bauble;
Let me never forget that the heinousness of sin lies
not so much in the nature of the sin committed,
as in the greatness of the Person sinned against.[1]

My long conversation with Carrie (see the beginning of chapter 4) stretched to over an hour. She waffled on her decision about whether to come with Jim for the intensive counseling workshop.

"I don't want to do this, Dr. Schaumburg! Everything within me wants to run away!" she said.

"Carrie, God has not given you answers to all the questions about Jim's sin and the misery you are in right now. But I have seen countless times, in situations much like yours, that God will not remain silent and He will show His power. I know this is hard to grab hold of, but this is the time to hate this evil in Jim with a passion."

"I do hate the evil, but I'm having trouble not hating him too."

"You know what Romans 12:21 says," I continued. "'Do not be overcome by evil, but overcome evil with good.' This is the exact moment when you can give Jim what he doesn't deserve—mercy and grace."

"You're right about that! He doesn't deserve anything from me! I still can't believe how he violated our marriage vows. I don't want him to ever touch me again. How could we have sex? All I would think about are those other women he's looking at and talking dirty with online!"

Our discussion continued in this vein for another thirty minutes. Eventually, Carrie said, "I do want what God wants. I talked to a woman who has been through your workshop and her situation was very much like mine. I know there is hope, but I'm scared that this will not work."

I didn't respond and waited for her decision.

"I know deep down I need to do it. I'll come."

As we start this chapter, I am continuing to build a foundation for understanding the need for sexual redemption. Such an understanding is important because this isn't a problem fixed through self-redemption, formulas, or a list of principles. We know by looking into our own hearts that we often sin sexually in our thoughts and attitudes, if not our actions. Most of us are aware that apart from God's grace, we would stand condemned in this area.

Sex!

We all respond to this word in different ways. While just a three-letter word, the fact is we all think about *it*, some of us are comfortable enough to talk about *it*, and frequently we joke about *it*.

There is not much else in life that causes more emotional pain, pleasure, passion, outrage, questions, confusion, anxiety, curiosity, abuse, exploitation, and violence on a personal and relational level than our sexuality and sex.

Sex has been around forever. It is of interest to everyone, regardless of socioeconomic status, cultural background, or education. And in spite of what younger people think, sex occupies our attention throughout our life span. Quite simply, sex is essential. And sex will not end until the new heaven and the new earth (see Luke 20:34–36).[2]

Married couples are supposed to engage in sex regularly, yet the truth is many do not and struggle sexually. Other couples use sex inappropriately in sinful ways. The way sex is viewed and worshiped in our culture is a perversion of the real importance of our sexuality.

In our day sex has come to mean an obsession with self and the body.

But the meaningfulness of sex is not found in a small dress size or flat abs. What are we trying to prove to ourselves? When it comes to trying to have the perfect body, I agree with Peyton Manning's priceless pep-talk advertisement for Mastercard: "Wish you had rock-hard abs? Look, I'm going to be honest—unless you are under the age of twenty-three or a professional football player, it's probably not going to happen. If I were you, I'd just buy bigger shirts!" The humor is in the truth of the statement and the foolishness of what we try to achieve with our bodies.

Sex certainly is about us and our bodies, but that's not the sum total of all that is sexual. Even in the church we miss the point. Biblically, the real significance of our sexuality is seen in creation, in intimacy, and even in our sinfulness. Yet it may surprise you that the overriding significance of our sexuality is ultimately found in the cross. If a husband holding his wife's hand looks into her eyes and whispers sweetly, "I want your body," and the wife as she squeezes his hand, gently kisses his cheek, and tenderly says, "I want you too," the meaning is crystal clear. In the same way, the cross brings union with Christ—one of the most fundamental teachings of the gospel. Through the Holy Spirit, we, *body and spirit*, have become one with Christ (1 Corinthians 6:15, 17; Ephesians 5:30). This union, and the future resurrection of the body, is God's bold statement that He wants your whole person, including your body. The cross and that sublime union give the Lord authority over your body, and He forbids giving your body to anyone other than your spouse (see 1 Corinthians 6:13b–20; 7:2–5).

While we get something of the impact of sex on human life, we need to go further and see our sexuality the way God sees it. The more we understand the truth about the significance of our sexuality, the better we will understand God and ourselves.

We Just Don't Get It

Sex is described and depicted in many ways. When scientific or clinical terms are used, sex almost sounds ho-hum. Simply put in physical terms, sex is concerned with activities involving the genitals and other body parts. Sexual *activity* not only produces physical feelings of pleasure, but may result in the creation of another human life.

Clinical descriptions are essential to sexual education, so they have their place. But we prefer something with a little more life. Even a kiss can be very sexual. Intercourse is a moment of passion, pleasure, union, and intimacy that brings an emotional, spiritual, and relational experience that could only have been designed by the infinite mind of an all-knowing God.

Given our passions, sexual attraction is typically an automatic plot element in films and novels. We men may not like "chick flicks" but even in an action flick we don't mind some romantic distraction. We all enjoy a good love story! We laugh and cry because the story stirs deep longings in us to have sexual satisfaction in a meaningful relationship. On the other hand, a graphic sex scene doesn't give us what we are truly looking for. Such displays don't take us to the higher level of meaning we desire, because they are full of misinformation about our sexuality. The movie scene can look nice, so well choreographed with just the right lighting, the right moves, and the right looks. Yet it's *not* real because those not-so-subtle messages tell you that sex is best and truly meaningful only for the young, beautiful, and athletic—and without long-term commitment.

As a counselor who has dealt for decades with human sexuality, let me tell you that message is false! The biblical truth about our sexuality is that sex should be meaningful to *every* married man and *every* married woman in good health regardless of age or physique.

The need for intimacy is ageless and the necessity for purity never ends. Sex may not be the same as it was in your twenties, but it can still be as fulfilling and enjoyable in later years. Regardless of what we see in our culture, body shape, size, and youthfulness are not what make sex good or significant. The real significance of sex is deeper, and the truth about our sexuality must be understood as a reflection of the union God desires to have with us in Christ.

Sex Begins at the Beginning

As we have seen, there is much more to our sexuality than physical activity and emotional experience. Sexuality is not some detached part of us, but is merged and incorporated into our total life for our entire lifetime.

Creation is basic to an understanding of our sexuality. Sexual distinction was created by God, and like it or not, God didn't create an androgynous being. There is a reason that Genesis doesn't say God created "human beings" or "human bodies" but rather "male and female he created them" (Genesis 1:27). In that distinctly clear statement sexuality is revealed as inherent in God's basic design, and the stage is set for fertility and the command to populate the earth (v. 28). We also note that these anatomically different bodies are both created "in His image." Therefore, every male and every female is created in God's image, so there is no qualitative difference between a man and a woman.

At the beginning we see that the basic reciprocating human relationship is between a man and a woman and it is sexual. Therefore, living, working, and being sexual are integral expressions that reflect the image of God. Thus we see that sex has a greater purpose than self-fulfillment.

Biblically, sexuality began the moment God created a man. Adam was no less a sexual being before Eve: he was fully male, a fully sexual being. The creation of a woman resulted in a whole new person and the ability for relational sexual fulfillment and procreation. We can assume that sexual activity began shortly after God presented Eve to Adam on their "wedding night." They were "naked and unashamed," which implies their contentment with something "very good."

From the beginning, godly sexuality was designed to be the contentment of one man with one woman for life. God's calling to lifelong exclusive sexual faithfulness is basic to understanding Adam and Eve's marriage and the order of God in marriage. I do not make that statement to condemn anyone. But to understand the true significance of sex, we must grieve the mess we have created.

Sexual Significance Is Found in Real Intimacy

Without God as the beginning point of sexuality, there is no more significance to the sexual intimacy of humans than of rodents (remember the research on voles?). Animals have sex by instinct, and we might act like animals at times, but that is not the way we are designed. "Making love" is an experience of losing yourself for the other; love requires giving or sacrificing of self. Each spouse loses themselves in the serving and pleasuring of the other. Today, the expression "making love" often refers only to sex.

Sex drive is not an animal instinct, strictly *dictated* by chemicals in the brain. "You were not meant to be led like a dog on the leash of lust or hunger."[3] We are made male and female in God's image, to seek to know and be known in the depth of human intimacy. Sin is never compatible with our union with Christ, and sexual sin is a unique offense against our own body, against our spouse, and against Christ. Paul says, "your bodies are members of Christ" (1 Corinthians 6:15). Our union with Christ is one of the apostle's most fundamental teachings, and this passage indicates that the union involves the whole person—the body as well as the soul. The error of the Corinthians was believing that what they did with their bodies did not affect their spiritual union. Through the Holy Spirit we have become one with Christ (1 Corinthians 6:17; Ephesians 5:30). We are not our own; our whole person belongs to Him, and we are His to possess and enjoy for His glory.

The drive to be sexual is more than simply a desire for pleasure or excitement. The sex drive is really a longing for closeness—in both sexes. Don't be fooled by false messages or even personal experience: men want closeness too. Every man that I have counseled who made his wife a sexual object, thereby giving the impression that all he wanted was sexual pleasure, has admitted—often with tears—that what he really wanted was closeness. This revelation was unbelievable to the wives who heard their husbands say that. It may seem unbelievable to you too—but it's true.

Sharing the pleasure of intimacy is the most satisfying human experience possible, and sexual pleasure reaches the highest level in a caring, loving, lifelong relationship. That's true because the most sexually excitable part of our body is our mind, and over time with one partner, the full, intimate connection of two hearts, souls, and bodies can occur.

All of us are sexual, yet it isn't always necessary to express our sexuality through intercourse. From personal experience and from counseling, I think two twenty-year-olds who can't keep their hands off each other have a lot to learn. It's possible that those of us over sixty have finally figured it out.

Sex isn't the only way to experience love and caring from our spouses, of course. As you grow older, you can give love to your spouse by caring, holding, caressing, hugging, and touching. Some years ago I was sitting in a small restaurant eating breakfast with a close friend. In my peripheral vision I saw an elderly couple awkwardly and carefully take their seats at a table next to ours. As they enjoyed their conversation and a morning out together, they were served their food and began to eat. The wife, in a caring voice, said to the husband who was struggling to raise his hand to get his food into his mouth, "Can I feed you?"

I had two thoughts: *God, don't ever let me be that old* (good luck with that desire) and *What an expression of love, passion, and intimacy. I've got a lot to learn in my marriage before I'm like that.*

So if you are growing older, enjoy each other. Focus on the pleasure you can give and receive, rather than on what used to be. We must work to never make sexual pleasure a means to a selfish end, a self-centered demand, but to see it as a spiritual, relational, and physical mutual experience for a married couple. And always remember that sex is a vital part of who we are as creatures made in His image. And as you age, an intimate, intense sexual union points to our future intense involvement with God in eternity. Late in life you appreciate more than ever what is great about your imperfect lover. "The shadow of covenant-keeping between husband and wife gives way to the reality of covenant-keeping between Christ and his glorified Church. Nothing is lost. The music of every pleasure is transposed into an infinitely higher key."[4] John Piper elaborates on the relationship between covenant and marriage as follows:

> The covenant-keeping love reached its climax in the death of Christ for his church, his bride. That death was the ultimate expression of grace, which is the ultimate expression of God's glory, which is of infinite value. Therefore, when Paul says that our great and final destiny is "the praise of [God's] glorious grace" (Eph. 1:6), he elevates marriage beyond measure, for here, uniquely, God displays the apex of the glory of his grace: "Christ loved the church and gave himself up for her" (Eph. 5:25).[5]

If you believe in the sovereignty of God, that God is both the Creator and Sustainer of life, you cannot think about sex or engage in sex without being aware of His divine presence. The beauty of marital intimacy created in the mind of God is often lost in our self-oriented culture that defines sex in private terms of what it can do for me, what it can do for my partner, or what it can do for our relationship. The significance of sex is far greater than that. We must begin to clearly see from the Word of God that marriage is for God's glory. Therefore I conclude that our sexuality is intended for God—His glory, His purposes, His service. Our sexuality—that is, our masculinity and femininity—as we will see in chapters 10 and 11, are to display God's glory. The covenant relationship of marriage, privately expressed in passionate sexual intimacy, and faithfully lived out publicly with one man and one woman, displays the covenant relationship of Christ and His church that will last forever. *We can tell the gospel story, but we can also live the gospel story.* Marriage is much more than being in love and having fulfilling sexual intimacy; it serves a greater purpose: It shows the truth of the gospel with our lives. It's not about perfect love, nor perfect sex. It is about the reality that, with all the pain, all the disappointment, and even with betrayal, there remains a covenant that puts on display the glory of the gospel.

The Loss of True Intimacy

Sadly, the innocent beauty of our sexuality was destroyed by the fall of Adam and Eve. The essence of the change caused by sin was a shift in our sexual intimacy from naked and unashamed (perfect intimacy) to naked and ashamed (imperfect intimacy). The man and woman went from living in perfect harmony to living under God's judgment.

While marriage is the only safe place for nakedness to occur, every time a man and a woman, in love and married, engage in meaningful sexual intimacy they are aware that something is wrong. The intimacy is real, but there is also a detectable uneasiness—a lack of confidence, a fear of inadequacy, or even a dread of potential rejection. So many married couples in describing their sexual relationship have indicated this struggle Carol, a pastor's wife, at age seventy-two, married forty-eight years, said, "For the better part of our marriage I felt we had a wonderful sex life. I would have liked more sex but did not insist on it." Rick, a thirty-six-year-old successful salesman, married thirteen years, put it this way: "I find Rene to be very attractive and desirable. She responds positively to me physically and enjoys our sex life. However, I have always struggled with initiating sexual activity. I fear rejection. I have never fully understood true intimacy." Tom and Phyllis, in their early twenties and married just over two years, struggled with sexual intimacy. "I'm very interested in sex with Phyllis and we make love almost every day. I try to be open to sexual intimacy, but I need to improve in this area." Phyllis said, "I'm open to sexual intimacy almost all of the time, unless I've been hurt." I could share many more examples. The names change, their ages, and the length of their marriages, and while each person enjoys sexual intimacy, each also indicates some level of concern that something just isn't right.

Complete comfort and security, which only Adam and Eve experienced, is absent. I often have wondered, *What was perfect intimacy like for that couple?* In our intimate relations we are weak and confused and sinfully choose false intimacy to avoid the reality of life in a fallen world. It's the same story I hear over and over again. Larry and Michelle get married and sexual passion seems to vanish overnight. There are many factors, from kids, to tiredness, to boredom, but their relationship is being lived outside the garden. Larry wants to be wanted; he wants his sexual advance to stir a deep response in Michelle, but she has the proverbial "headache." Inwardly, like every man, Larry wants to avoid rejection, so he holds back initiating sex and chooses to get out of bed after Michelle falls asleep and go to the world of false intimacy on the computer where his "advances" will always be accepted. Human sexuality, with its feelings and behaviors, is tragically damaged and more fragile than we like to admit.

The fall did not change the physical act between a man and woman, but it drastically impacts our ability to keep it holy and satisfying. Perverted sexual desire is a powerful force in turning us away from godly sex. Here's how the apostle Paul described that power:

> *God gave them up* in the lusts of their hearts to impurity, to the dishonoring of their bodies among themselves. . . . *God gave them up* to dishonorable passions. For women exchanged natural relations for those that are contrary to nature; and the men likewise gave up natural desires with women and were consumed with passion for one another, men committing shameless acts with men. . . . *God gave them up* to a debased mind to do what ought not to be done. (Romans 1:24–28)

We first pervert our instinct to put God first, and the consequence is the domination of lust. What is natural desire disintegrates, and there is a bondage to uncontrolled passions. Simply put, God's restraints are removed. Yet, we are always culpable and therefore under God's wrath (see 1 Corinthians 6:9–10).

Twisting the instinct to put God first is a perversion of our sexuality and the consequence is degradation of our body and our sexuality. Perverted sex is the most powerful force over the human will because it not only distorts our human nature, but also changes our understanding of the reality of God's sovereignty. We may say that God is Lord of the universe, and then turn right around and do what we want with our bodies. This disregard for God leads to a disregard for others. Lust always leaves victims because in sexual sin everyone gets hurt.

We should not lose sight of the real issue, however: Sexual sin attacks God Himself. When we sin sexually, we make God our enemy. Sexual sin is a violation of our bodies, and thus a violation of the image of God. Just as desecrating the statute of the king in the town square was considered a violation of the king himself, so violation of the image of God is a gross act of disobedience.

Within all sin there lies a choice. Adam chose to listen to his wife rather than trust and obey God. He fully knew what he was doing, in effect preferring a relationship with a woman, including their sexual intimacy, over the meaningful relationship he had established with God. As with Adam, choosing sex over God always impacts our relationship with God, as well as our future spiritual existence: "Neither the sexually immoral . . . nor adulterers, nor men who practice homosexuality . . . will inherit the kingdom of God" (1 Corinthians 6:9–10).

Sexual purity is God-centered, sexual sin is self-centered. Sexual sin always leads people away from God, in this life, and in the life to come.

With such potential in our sexuality for evil, we might ask why God created us as sexual beings in the first place.

Why Do We Have a Body?

The therapeutic culture might suggest we have a body because God is relational and He created us primarily for meaningful relationships with others. I think that's partly right but very misleading. In deepening our understanding of why sexual sin is such a big deal, the proper question to start with is, Why do we have a body?

There are really only two views. The secular view, the view that doesn't acknowledge God, maintains the body counts for nothing but self-fulfillment and I can do what I want with it. Or, the biblical view, which even some Christians don't understand, that the body is "for the Lord, and the Lord for the body" (1 Corinthians 6:13b). If there is any doubt in our minds, one only has to read the next sentence: "And God raised the Lord and will also raise us up by his power" (v. 14). Paraphrased: God wants your body and He is coming to get it. And as Paul goes on to say in the rest of the chapter, you can't do just anything you want with your body.

Hebrews 13:4, "Let marriage be held in honor among all, and let the marriage bed be undefiled," is properly understood when we see the truth about our sexuality and spirituality and that there is an even more holy union with the Lord. A married couple torn apart by unfaithfulness, paralyzed by mistrust, and with much sorrow and great pain have only taken the first step when they seek to reconcile their marriage to avoid divorce or keep from damaging their children. They must learn to see that the greatest violation is against their covenant union with Christ. Our union with the Lord requires a higher level of purity and fidelity. In union with the Lord we become "one spirit with him" (1 Corinthians 6:17). There is an inner, and very real, spiritual union with the Lord. *Yet we must not fail to remember that union with Christ involves the body.*

The dignity of the body, with its destiny, comes at a price. And it wasn't cheap! The Lord wants your body, the Spirit lives in your body, and your body isn't really yours! We foolishly think our body belongs to us. No, it's "not your own" (1 Corinthians 6:19). I can't take what belongs to someone else and use it without permission. If you take my truck without my permission, you're in big trouble. And neither can you take your body, which isn't yours, and use it in sexual sin without permission.

Of course, God will never give you permission under any circumstance. And don't forget, God isn't paying on credit—it's a done deal! Paul explains this truth with the metaphor of slavery (see 1 Corinthians 7:22–23). All true believers are bought to do God's will, not our own. The body, not just your spirit, not just your mind, was included in the purchase. Sexual redemption starts with being bought; without that purchase there can be no sexual redemption.

The lie from the beginning, and rampant in our age, is that we can do what we want—we have the right! No, we are slaves. In the truest sense there is no autonomous freedom. Either we are "slaves to impurity and to lawlessness leading to more lawlessness" (Romans 6:19), or we are "slaves to righteousness leading to sanctification." This is our true freedom: "But now that you have been set free from sin and have become slaves of God, the fruit you get leads to sanctification and its end, eternal life" (Romans 6:22).

The biblical view results in just one choice: Choose God over our selfish sexual desires. If we do, then we must let God forgive us of our past sexual sins. We must let God give us the power to master sexuality in holiness. We must choose the perfect will of God, and not be led astray by promises of false intimacy.

Romans 8:12–13 says, "So then, brothers, we are debtors, not to the flesh, to live according to the flesh. For if you live according to the flesh you will die, but if by the Spirit you put to death the deeds of the body, you will live." Paul is saying that if you understand that your body is the Lord's, you have life; if not, you will die. The choice is extremely important! Even our desire for sexual intimacy, properly understood, teaches us to search after God *in faith* with all our heart, mind, and body. As John Piper explains, "If [sexual] gratification is not denied us but offered to us in marriage, we will seek it and enjoy it only in ways that reflect our faith. To put it another way, while the contentment of faith does not put an end to our hunger, weariness, or sexual appetite, it does transform the way we go about satisfying those desires."[6] The fact of our ownership by Christ as His slave compels us to satisfy our desires only in the way that pleases Him and brings Him glory.

To answer the original question, Why do you have a body? the biblical answer is to "glorify God in your body" (1 Corinthians 6:20).

One Flesh

In all the years that I have counseled married couples and seen the never ending struggle with sexual intimacy and false intimacy, I'm convinced that we understand very little about "one flesh." Two primary indicators that this is true are the existence of sexual immorality in marriage and the prevalence of divorce.

The truth about our sexuality is that when any man or woman engages in sexual intercourse, it's a one-flesh *act*. And, when a couple mutually consents to marriage, they enter a one-flesh *relationship*.

The mystery of one flesh in marriage points to *the* Mystery, so deeply profound, that we, the enemies of God, are made one with the Son of God. As a result, any unfaithfulness, by whatever name, from premarital sex to prostitution, distorts the representation our lives should be of God's oneness with us. The oneness is ultimately about Christ and us, but Paul makes this application of it to marriage: "Let each one of you love his wife as himself, and let the wife see that she respects her husband" (Ephesians 5:33). In everything that a godly man does in his God-honoring leadership, the wife is to respond to; and the husband is to sacrificially love and serve his wife.

Today in the church we are losing a biblical faith that guides our outlook on sexuality and determines how we think and behave sexually. I conclude that no formula, no technique, and no twelve-step program will help us recover such a faith. In fact, such strategies for sexual recovery will distract us from the solution.

We need sexual redemption.

The Path to Sexual Redemption

1 Ponder the reality that your femininity or masculinity reflects the image of God.

2 "The body is not meant for sexual immorality, but for the Lord, and the Lord for the body" (1 Corinthians 6:13b). Have you fully recognized the noble purpose for which God has given you a body?

3 Union with Christ is incompatible with sexual sin, so consider that sexual union has a spiritual component: That a sexual act outside of marriage is a unique sin against the Lord's body, and against your body that belongs to Christ (1 Corinthians 6:13–20). The inverse is also true: Sexual union within marriage is to have a positive spiritual significance. Therefore, what needs to change spiritually and sexually in your life?

CHAPTER SIX

The Missing Male

I desire to conquer self in every respect,
to overcome the body with its affections and lusts,
to keep under my flesh,
to guard my manhood from all grosser sins,
to check the refined power of my natural mind,
to live entirely to thy glory,
to be deaf to unmerited censure and praise of men.
I wish not so much to do as to be,
and I long to be like Jesus;
If thou dost make me right I shall be right;
Lord, I belong to thee,
make me worthy of thyself.[1]

I met with Carrie and Jim for the first time on a Wednesday morning in my counseling office. They both looked pretty rough. My hunch was that they had done a lot of tossing and turning during a largely sleepless night.

I have a small sitting area furnished with three comfortable chairs separated by a small end table, and furnished with water bottles and a large box of tissue. We exchanged handshakes and after they were seated, we dove in. Smiling, I asked them, "Well, who wants to plunge in first?"

Carrie looked at Jim, but he averted his eyes and dropped his head. She said sharply through tight lips, "I think he should go first! Wouldn't that make sense, Dr. Schaumburg?"

I didn't respond. During this first time together, my primary goal is to assess their condition as individuals and as a couple. Any and all data is instructive. Typically, if it's the man who's been caught in a sexual indiscretion, the wife is very eager to get her husband to admit everything and get the process of "fixing him and his awful problem" underway. Or, she may be hanging by a thread, ready to drop out of the counseling workshop at any time and put her husband in the rearview mirror.

Jim looked helplessly at me and said, "Well, I guess I need to say something. I never thought I would end up where I'm at. I sure never wanted to hurt Carrie or cause all these problems for my family and everyone." He paused and looked mournfully at me again. He also shot a quick sideglance at Carrie. She was looking straight ahead, legs tightly crossed, her fingers nervously picking at the paper label on her water bottle. I could tell she was fighting to hold back tears, but she blurted out, "How could you treat me like this; what were you thinking?" I ignored her words and emotions for the moment and turned to look at Jim. I could tell that for Jim this was embarrassing and excruciatingly painful.

Jim cleared his throat and went on. "I first discovered some pornographic magazines hidden in the garage when I was eleven years old. I was pretty naive about things, so at first the pictures almost scared me. I also felt ashamed. I knew there was something bad about those magazines and my dad, I guess, had tried to hide them. So I put them away and got out of there fast. But I thought about the pictures and wondered what else was in those magazines. So I started sneaking out there more and more to look. I liked looking at naked women. That's where it began. And I guess I got hooked then."

Jim's story of how he got enticed by pornography is typical, particularly for men who grew up before the proliferation of the Internet. His eyes were captivated by photos of a woman's nakedness. All men are visual (women too). Men acting in the selfishness of their hearts are notoriously visual in their sexual sin whether it's lust, pornography, lap dances, adultery, or prostitution. That being true, what more could we learn about masculine sexuality fed by a deceitful heart?

Believe me, a lot.

This chapter is especially for men, but I want every woman to read it as well. (I will urge the same thing at the beginning of the next chapter focused on women.) In chapter 10 I will suggest what we men need to do to improve the situation related to our sexuality, but before we get there I want to talk more pointedly about what seems to have gone wrong from the inside out.

Books, seminars, and conferences on masculinity abound. And when it comes to the issue of lust, doesn't every man understand our problem by now?

Women certainly think they do. Get a hundred women together, and a hundred of them will probably agree on the nature of the male sex drive: "It's pretty much all he thinks about and wants!" Yet in all my years of analysis, I repeatedly find that there is still much misinformation and misunderstanding about male sexuality and, in particular, how a man's sexuality relates to his spirituality. Why is there so much confusion?

Are Men Relational?

In my experience as a man and in ministering to men, I find men quite relational—much more so than understood by conventional wisdom. Granted, this desire to connect can be hidden from everyone, including ourselves. But here's a clue to finding men's relational drive: All men want to be respected. Of course, men want to be loved too, but our path to feeling loved is first to receive respect for who we are as a man. A man is always looking for intimacy in the expression of respect from his wife.

Finding significant respect is not easy. First, all of us men standing before a woman in a fallen world start out feeling naked and ashamed, even with our clothes on. There is a built-in fear of being inadequate. We may not act like it, but believe me at some level our thought is, *Can I measure up as a man?*

In one way or another, subtly or not so subtly, someone—sometimes our wives—will say to us, "Well, if you want to be respected, why don't you act like a man?" Ouch! Maybe that's a fair question, but the challenge to be a man in a fallen world is daunting. As his forefather Adam found out after the horrendous rebellion in the garden, every man encounters pain and frustration. Not every guy plows a field, but we all feel the pain and frustration in our labor—whether it's our marriage, family, or job.

If every effort I put forth comes with some pain and frustration, when, where, and how can I expect to consistently find respect? It is not possible, and God designed it that way for a reason! Thousands of times I have wanted to make it all happen in love, in parenting, and in service to God. And yet it feels like ninety-nine times out of a hundred my effort is painfully frustrated and all that I want as a man is beyond my grasp.

In 1999 we started renting and living on a beautiful property where we operated our counseling workshop. The plan was to purchase this ideal setting, but we were turned down forty times on loan applications. Since in the first place God had made the property available so miraculously, this was a huge, confusing frustration to me! I felt as if I'd flown a small plane into a box canyon and the walls were getting closer and closer to the wingtips. With no room to turn around, disaster was certain.

At that point it was easy to question my initial decision, my leadership ability, my motives, and even my masculinity. I wanted to wallow in self-pity. The way I viewed this, crashing and burning wouldn't be all bad, because at one level I wanted to die to get out of the mess! My deeper fear was that everyone would find out that I was a foolish man who had no idea what he was doing. On top of that, my wife, Rosemary, probably would never follow me again on any other "hair-brained" idea.

With that type of fear raging inside of a man, what is the ungodly response from a deceitful masculine heart? Discouragement, anger, and self-pity are followed by a stubborn attempt to not feel the pain and frustration *again*. And in spite of reality to find some *respect*, or at least to make every effort to avoid *disrespect*. When I respond this way I not only become less of a man, but even more significantly, God is not glorified in my masculinity.

Specifically, when we men battle to overcome our fears, we become less sensitive in our relationships—we act like we could care less. We withdraw because we just don't want to hurt anymore. We back away from leadership in our marriage and in the family. In short, we become the classic male wimp. No wonder our wives get frustrated and feel justified when taking more control.

A man stuck in this place will often feel like a child with his wife and may become sexually impotent with her. Or he may run into the arms of another woman who gives what appears to be respect, but is nothing but false intimacy. Outside his marriage he will look and act more like an adult than a child, be it looking at a sexual image on the Internet, having a one-night stand, visiting a prostitute, or finding a lover. In that phony world, his masculinity appears vital, but it's only an illusion.

In my counseling office I frequently hear the relational distortion, the rebellion, the self-deception, and the stubbornness: "*This* woman wants me, and my wife doesn't. She doesn't respect me, but the other woman does." It doesn't look or smell like it, but under all his foolishness, each and every man wants a meaningful relationship the way God designed it. But his deceitful heart has led him astray.

Some men hide their fear, pain, and frustration behind a *visible* arrogance because they believe they can handle it their way. Along with the anger comes an assertiveness, aggressiveness, and tyrannical demand that his wife do things his way. "Don't you dare resist me!" he says. Sexually, this man may be too busy for sex with his wife, but when he wants sex, she better comply or she'll pay.

Other men hide the pain and frustration behind a *quiet* arrogance. The anger is deep inside as they run life their way. They would never confront or impose on anyone, and often never initiate sex with their wife or any woman, always leaving it to the woman to make the first move. Both types of arrogant men are wide-open to sexual temptation or sexual dysfunction. Spiritually, both men provide very little in terms of spiritual nurture and protection.

Years ago a wife came to me for help. Her husband was a successful physician, but a weak man. She had lost interest in having sex with him because of his lack of true masculinity. Rather than becoming a man and a true lover and having her respond as a woman, he bargained with her: "Agree to have sex with me every night for three months and I'll buy you that new BMW." If it wasn't a new car, it was a European vacation, new furniture, or more jewelry. He believed the lie that he didn't have what it took in and of himself to be respected and loved. Foolishly, he believed the things she wanted would be a way to get what he wanted. This only increased her hurt and the disgust she felt for him.

Misunderstanding Men

While I was writing this chapter, a man called me for help. He explained that his problem of looking at women had led to an emotional affair with a much younger coworker. The relationship had almost become physical. He had confessed this dalliance to his wife who was now beside herself with fear that she might lose her husband because she thinks she can't compete with a younger woman.

Because of misinformation, the man is only addressing the symptom of the problem—his wandering eyes—instead of the root problem. His strategy is to attempt to look away every time he sees a young, good-looking woman, to keep boundaries in his relationships at work, and to pay more attention to his wife. After several months he is experiencing moderate success. Naively, he thinks he is doing much better, primarily because the young woman recently left town.

I suggest, however, that looking the other way, not spending time alone with this woman, and pursuing a better relationship with his wife are woefully inadequate responses. If the core problem has not been dealt with, the cancer in his heart will roar out of remission and overwhelm him at some point when a young woman comes along and pays attention to him. Protection from unfaithfulness is not primarily found in identifying the triggers, forming the right attitudes, evaluating the risk factors in a relationship, or establishing contracts with your spouse on handling an attraction to someone else. Everything we do relationally with the opposite sex or even the same sex *must* address the internal disposition of the heart.

The confusion starts when we carelessly assume that men are not naturally created to link sex with love—that only women can do that. I believe this assumption about men results from too much focus on the behavior of sinful men, not by observing godly men or from a careful reading of Scripture. Somehow we have come to believe that the pervasiveness of lustful looking is natural even for a true believer, and that every man *naturally* looks with "lustful intent" (Matthew 5:28) at the sight of a woman's body. What is natural, for both men and women, is to notice *all* forms of beauty, including the beauty of the opposite sex. But sinful lust is a sexual desire that sins against God and dishonors the person lusted after. Abnormal male behavior is now so frequent that we call it normal. Then we actually blame God because He made men with the capacity to admire a woman's beauty.

I counseled a fifty-year-old pastor who visited an eighty-year-old widow shortly after conducting her husband's funeral. In her need to be held, she was vulnerable, in his need to be respected, so was he. Their sexual affair wasn't based on visual attraction. The pastor's wife could not comprehend the visual attraction of an eighty-year-old woman. Believing the woman must be the most physically attractive octogenarian alive, the pastor's wife knocked on her door to prove her perception of the problem. She was shocked to find a wrinkled old lady answering the door. Lustful intent is not inherently visual; it is of the heart, not the eyes, with an intent to take and to use for sexual pleasure without regard for the whole person.

Then the issue of lusting eyes is taken a step further and blame is placed on a man's brain chemicals. These assumptions are mistaken: Every individual, man or woman, has the God-given aptitude to appreciate the beauty of a flower, a sunset, and another person. That's natural to both sexes. Lust is *not* the same thing as the pleasure and enjoyment of inner beauty that God designed men and women to appreciate. Lust is a desire for fading physical beauty (versus "unfading beauty") with a self-serving purpose. It is a disregard for God and the other person.

God didn't create us to sinfully look, any more than I am tempted by God to sin: "Let no one say when he is tempted, 'I am being tempted by God,' for God cannot be tempted with evil, and he himself tempts no one" (James 1:13). Sin is natural for an unredeemed person, but as a man made in the Creator's image and re-created through the cross into His likeness, sin can be overcome. As Paul wrote, "You have put off the old self with its practices and have put on the new self, which is being renewed in knowledge after the image of its creator" (Colossians 3:9–10).

We get even more confused in our understanding of men when we talk about them lusting after a woman's body more than a woman lusts after a man's body. It is true that with the speed of light a man can look at a woman with lustful intent. But it's his wicked heart and mind that are the problem, not some hardwired propensity or a brain chemical. Deep within a man made in God's image there is a desire for meaningful relationship. It's his self-centered, self-deceived heart that leads him to pursue relationships based on lust and what is actually fading beauty.

Yes, a man can move from wanting a relationship to wanting sex to wanting a relationship with lightning speed. But in this blur, don't overlook a man's relational desire: it's just as real as a woman's. Ask any thoughtful man and he will tell you that deep down he really doesn't want sex if the woman doesn't really want him relationally.

Men take sex from a prostitute but not for the reasons we assume—that men are visual and naturally wired to want it from any woman. Rather the truth is that men are foolish, which points to the real problem—the wicked heart and mind. Even knowing that the prostitute is lying about appreciating and wanting him, the man pays for sex to experience the illusion of relational intimacy. In fact, many men turn away from a prostitute's offer of sex if the woman can't do a good job of lying about wanting authentic intimacy.

A husband, acting somewhat like the man going to a prostitute, will take sex from his disinterested wife for the sake of false intimacy. But in reality he hates that kind of response from his wife.

Heart Problems

If sexual redemption is our true need, a natural question is, "What is it specifically that requires sexual redemption?" We must always remember in looking at men (and women too) what the real problem is: "The heart is deceitful above all things, and desperately sick; who can understand it?" (Jeremiah 17:9). Jesus was clearly concerned about this heart problem:

> You have heard that it was said, "You shall not commit adultery." But I say to you that everyone who looks at a woman with lustful intent has already committed adultery with her in his heart. If your right eye causes you to sin, tear it out and throw it away. For it is better that you lose one of your members than that your whole body be thrown into hell. And if your right hand causes you to sin, cut it off and throw it away. For it is better that you lose one of your members than that your whole body go into hell. (Matthew 5:27–30)

In fact, behavior that is really good can only come out of a transformed heart, not Christian behavioral management, new techniques, recovery, or effective resolution of our past. Jesus said that the heart is the problem: "For you clean the outside of the cup and the plate, but inside they are full of greed and self-indulgence" (Matthew 23:25).

The outward behavior is the symptom of the problem. So many writers, counselors, pastors, and teachers deal with symptom relief. When they address sexual sin, it's solely as an addiction or a disease, even when they use the words "sin" and "addiction" in the same sentence.

They may also declare that a sexual sin is a demonic attack, then add the disease concept to further define the problem and point to solutions. Certainly, Satan is our adversary, an accuser, and tempter; so he is dangerous. As Peter said, "Be sober-minded; be watchful. Your adversary the devil prowls around like a roaring lion, seeking someone to devour. Resist him, firm in your faith" (1 Peter 5:8–9). The truth is, however, that even with all of his power and tricks, Satan can't make you and me sin. When we say, "The devil made me do it," that's not true! Past experiences, good and bad, shape us, but they don't dictate or make us do what's wrong.

We cannot forget what Jesus taught: "out of the heart come evil thoughts, murder, adultery, sexual immorality, theft, false witness, slander'" (Matthew 15:19).

The devil must be dealt with, and our past is significant. But in a crisis, go for the jugular of sin: *Ask God to look on the inside, to search the heart, and get to the core of what's going on in your life.* The proper posture of a sexual sinner is modeled for us in David. First, he understands whom he has sinned against. "Against you, you only, have I sinned and done what is evil in your sight" (Psalm 51:4). Second, he recognizes his need for mercy and the one who gives it. "Have mercy on me, O God, according to your steadfast love; according to your abundant mercy blot out my transgressions" (Psalm 51:1). Third, he knows that God has to do the work. "Wash me thoroughly from my iniquity and cleanse me from my sin" (Psalm 51:2)! David knew after sinning with Bathsheba that the redirection of his sinful desires and actions could only come through the intervention of God.

Sanctification always begins with God's work. Having passed from spiritual death to life, growth in sanctification, in this case sexual purity, is an ongoing process that is dependent on God's continuous work in the heart of the believer, and also requires the believer's continuous struggle against sin. The process is neither self-reliant labor nor God-reliant passivity. In other words, overcoming sexual sin is human effort dependent on God (see 2 Corinthians 7:1; Philippians 3:10–14; Hebrews 12:14).

We are powerless over our sexual behaviors and thoughts without His mercy and grace, but the problem is much bigger. We can't even *want to change* unless God shows mercy. "He has mercy on whomever he wills, and he hardens whomever he wills" (Romans 9:18). Mercy is God's prerogative; we need His good pleasure. When that work begins with a heart opened to His complete will, we will continue to pray, as David did, "Create in me a clean heart, O God, and renew a right spirit within me. Cast me not away from your presence, and take not your Holy Spirit from me. Restore to me the joy of your salvation, and uphold me with a willing spirit" (Psalm 51:10–12). The cross addresses our deepest need, which is not to escape the bondage and hurt from our past, but instead to remove the crud on the inside that defiles every man and woman. In later chapters I will look at the details of our responsibility in response to His initial mercy.

When you change the inside of your life through sexual redemption, the outside will change, too, but it is the fruit of real change on the inside. Sexual redemption is a deeper work because it instills a righteousness of the heart rather than a successful averting of the eyes, a good accountability partner, working the steps, having a plan of protection, or escaping a dysfunctional family. Even having more intimacy in marriage isn't the full answer, because intimacy must have the right ultimate purpose of God's glory, of putting the "gospel reality on display in the world. That is why we are married. That is why all married people are married, even when they don't know and embrace the gospel."[2]

Heart Impotence

All the ads for Cialis, Levitra, and Viagra have gone from vague to vulgar, with parents having to try to answer a five-year-old daughter's question like, "Daddy, what's a 'four-hour erection?'" This truly is madness motivated by greed. When Pfizer released its new impotence drug, Viagra, Wall Street analysts had already estimated that the medicine could easily hit sales of $6 billion or even $11 billion a year.[3] What infuriates me is that the drug manufacturers, and most men, don't want to know what was happening spiritually and relationally *before* they had erectile dysfunction. While impotence is a medical problem 80 to 90 percent of the time,[4] erectile dysfunction can also be a symptom of a deep-seated masculine heart problem. A pill can't fix a heart problem that involves spiritual, sexual, and relational factors.

Just as clogged arteries can cause chest pain, the deceitful masculine heart produces recognizable symptoms that should not be ignored. Non-medical erectile dysfunction is a clue revealing an impotence in the masculine heart. For some men this heart impotence expresses itself sexually. For others it comes out in relational impotence. And for a number of men it shows up in spiritual weakness and the lack of male leadership in the home.

Rich owned his own company and had over two hundred employees. At work he was a take-charge guy who decisively led a successful business. At home it was a different story. His wife, Jan, was a stay-at-home mom who kept the house and family in order. With five children, Rich felt like the sixth child around his controlling wife. But Jan felt like she had not just five children but a husband who behaved like the sixth kid.

In counseling, as Rick grappled with his unfaithfulness before God in the form of pornography use, he started to understand the depth of deceit in his own heart. He explained his symptoms, which are common in many men, this way: "When my kids ask me to come outside and play, eager to be a good dad, I say yes. The second question they ask is, 'Do we need coats on?' I always say, 'Go ask your mom.' I do this after learning that I could never get it right. If they had coats on, she would yell from the back door, 'Why do those kids have coats on, it's too warm out there!' If they didn't have coats on she would yell, 'Why don't they have coats on, it's too cold out there!' Either way I felt like an incompetent child."

Rick wasn't just trying to cooperate and keep the peace; he was avoiding looking incompetent by not making a simple decision and being accountable for it. In so doing, he was more concerned with protecting himself and his good image than demonstrating leadership.

What does the man's symptom of feeling like a child and his wife feeling like she has an extra kid point to? Looking at one side of the relationship, to put it bluntly, such a man is a wimp and coward. He feels both shame and guilt in his failed role, but resents his wife's control. Looking at the other side of the same coin, the wife is a controlling witch, hates herself for being like that, resents her husband's failure to lead, but justifies her response because she believes he will never change. In the final analysis, the buck stops with the God-given role of leadership, so he must own the fact that his weakness appears to justify disregarding God and others in order to look out for numero uno.

The Missing Male

How did we get into this mess? Rather than looking at our parents and our family history, let's go much further back, to the beginning. Many biblical scholars note that in creating "man in his own image . . . male and female" (Genesis 1:27), that they were to "subdue" and were given "dominion . . . over every living thing that moves on the earth" (v. 28). Instead, they betrayed the trust placed in them and in an act of treachery rebelled and obeyed one of God's creatures (the serpent). I agree with the idea that Eve, being deceived and taking the first bite, didn't actually start the process of the fall. Rather, it was Adam not challenging the craftiest creature on the planet when it showed up (Genesis 3:1). Adam's sin cannot be overemphasized. His sin was a conscious act of rebellion and he failed to carry out his God-ordained responsibility to guard or "keep" (Genesis 2:15). An egalitarian view would disagree, but Adam, under the command of God (see Genesis 2:16), was to carry out leadership responsibility to care for his wife, Eve. Therefore, I believe you can build a case for the argument that the first step in the fall was Adam's failure to lead, and from then until the present, we men stubbornly continue to follow him right into our own foolishness.

Adam sinned in not following the command of God: "And the Lord God commanded the man [in the absence of Eve],[5] saying, 'You may surely eat of every tree of the garden, but of the tree of the knowledge of good and evil you shall not eat, for in the day that you eat of it you shall surely die'"

(Genesis 2:16–17). When God later caught up with Adam and Eve after the fall, He "called to the man . . . , 'Where are you?'" (Genesis 3:9)[6] and then asked Adam three questions related to his record as a leader and let him give his lame excuse:

- "Where are you?"(Genesis 3:9)
- "Who told you that you were naked?" (Genesis 3:11)
- "Have you eaten of the tree of which I commanded you not to eat?" (Genesis 3:11)

Reminiscent of the response of men ever since, Adam denied his leadership responsibility and blamed the woman, a distinct failure of courage that put his relationship with God and his wife at risk.

I can imagine what Eve might have said to Adam after God left the scene of the crime: "What were you thinking? When are you going to take some responsibility around here?" Maybe she felt like a mother who already had a little boy—before Cain and Abel were born. I think it's quite reasonable to assume that on that first night out of the garden, Adam slept outside the tent! She didn't invite him in, and I doubt he even attempted to sleep with her. At the same time, when confronted by the serpent, she didn't turn to Adam for direction or protection. She did what she wanted to do and got her husband to go along with her plan. Some things never change!

But Adam's pathetic weakness really surfaced when in an attempt to exonerate himself, he suggested that maybe it really was God who was to blame because He was the one who put "this woman" in the garden in the first place.

At this point it's as if God has a "you've got to be kidding" response and without comment turns His attention to Eve, asking her, "What is this that you have done?" (Genesis 3:13). Eve, too, even though she'd played a role in the rebellion against God, tried to wiggle out of responsibility by trying to shift blame onto the serpent. God then chooses not to respond to her immediately, either. When He does address Eve directly, He speaks judgment on the woman.

The interaction between God and this couple vividly shows how from the very beginning the deceitful heart—both Adam's and Eve's—tried to make excuses and shift blame. Both hearts reverse the created order of God, as John Hartley points out in his commentary on Genesis: "The woman acted in harmony with the man, rather than an individual set apart from him. This is visible in her use of plural forms of speaking for both of them. The serpent likewise used plural forms in addressing the woman. Thus no scene recounts the woman's seeking to influence the man to eat; they were in total accord."[7] However, as indicated above, a case can be made that Adam declined to take leadership in resisting Satan and by "listening" to Eve. By following her instructions he removed himself from God's authority and put himself under his wife's guidance. (I believe, and will argue the point later, that men have the greater responsibility for the sexual, relational, and spiritual quality of the marriage.)

Back to the Genesis story. God ignored the responses of both the man and the woman and immediately moved to punish and curse the serpent without even dignifying it by asking a question or allowing it to speak: "The Lord God said to the serpent, 'Because you have done this, cursed are you . . .'" (Genesis 3:14). A curse is the opposite of a blessing. In Eden, what was will now never be again without God's redemptive intervention.

As some commentators[8] point out, God "cursed" the serpent and the ground (Genesis 3:14, 17), but the word is not used directly with the man and the woman. He did inflict judgment/punishment in the form of pain for both women and men exactly where it hurts: In sustaining life, having children, and producing food. (Later, we will see that His judgment has a long-range purpose for the glory of God, but I'm jumping ahead in the story.) The judgment comes first for the woman in procreation, and then for the man in his need to work hard to provide for himself and his family.

Nothing has changed since then: Pain—physical and emotional—come where we attempt to sustain life and make it work. Life is subject to futility and frustration in our sexuality (naked and ashamed), in our relationships (leadership exists, but leadership is imperfect), in finding meaningful purpose and fulfillment (pain in procreation and constant weeds), and finally life comes to an end in the horror of death and dying.

God's redemptive intervention is the only living hope if we are to cease being missing men who abandon our God-given role of leadership. God's work of grace is a calling to live for God's purpose. A godly man, living out the redemption of his masculinity, is guided more by the Word of God than his own wisdom. He is a man who takes responsibility and strives to meet the needs of others rather than seeking his own immediate pleasures. His wife and others do not see him as demanding his own way but offering guidance and direction. He steps into difficult challenges, not just at work, but spiritually and relationally in his marriage and family. He is not wishy-washy, but decisive; thus he acts on his God-given instincts to protect and to take the initiative relationally and sexually. This is the man whose wife finds comfort and reassurance in his strength.

The Path to Sexual Redemption

1 In what area of your life do you feel frustration? Do you feel like a child? Like a mother?

2 Do you agree or disagree with the idea that what you want most in your relationship with your wife is respect and a meaningful relationship?

3 In your relationships and role as a leader, in what ways do you feel you are a "missing male"?

4 Do you find yourself avoiding conflict and failing to take the initiative sexually, relationally, and spiritually?

CHAPTER SEVEN

The Hardened Female

O that all my distresses and apprehensions
might prove but Christ's school
to make me fit for greater service
by teaching me the great lesson of humility.[1]

In my face-to-face interview with Jim and Carrie, Jim paused in telling his story for a sip from his water bottle. I wondered for a moment whether he would say anything else without prompting, so I offered some encouragement by nodding my head and smiling.

"I kept looking at the magazines and when I got into high school I bought some of my own," Jim said. "Now I was really feeling my own sex drive and could not help it and, uh, would masturbate when I looked at the pictures.

"When I got to college there was a lot of porn around and nobody really cared, so I just looked at it whenever I felt like it . . . which was pretty often. When I was a junior I had a serious girlfriend, and we did some stuff with each other, so I didn't use the porn so much then. It was before I met Carrie . . ." Jim paused and once again glanced at his wife. She was dabbing her eyes and did not acknowledge him.

"I broke up with that girl. I met Carrie a couple of years later. Our relationship was pretty physical, from fondling to oral sex. So while we were dating I did okay again and I thought that once we got married I wouldn't have the problem anymore. I always wanted to stop. I would pray and ask

God to help me and vow I would never do it again. I don't know how many times I threw my magazines away.

"It would be okay for a while, but then I would be tempted on a business trip to buy a magazine or watch a movie in the hotel. And I'd get right back into it. I'm really sorry about this." While saying that Jim looked first at me, then glanced toward Carrie. Again, she did not acknowledge him at all. There were a few moments of awkward silence. I smiled and took a sip from my water bottle. Jim had more.

"I know what's really bad, with Carrie and me, is the second thing . . . I, uh, after she saw on my laptop I'd been to some porn sites, I confessed. But I didn't tell her . . ." Jim trailed off. He looked at Carrie again. She was now crying harder. Eyes red and cheeks puffy, she reached for another handful of tissue. He continued, his voice so soft I could barely hear him, "She really lost it—I can't blame her that much—when she found the emails to the girls—women—I met in a chat room."

I decided to gently intervene. "Thanks, Jim, for bringing me up to date," I said, and then directed my attention to Carrie. "Carrie, listening to Jim telling this and revealing how unfaithful he's been, how does this affect you?"

Her voice cracking, Carrie answered, "I still can't believe it! I can't get over the fact that this is the man I married and trusted all these years! He's been a good father and we've taught Sunday school and everything, and now *this*! I'm devastated." She finally looked at Jim. It was not a pleasant face. There was a hardness that said *Never will you hurt me again!*

Carrie was deeply wounded by her husband's unfaithfulness. Her trust in him was broken and she wondered how she could ever even consider physical intimacy with him again. And perhaps worst of all, now she had to deal with her own hardening heart.

Before I begin this chapter on a woman's sexuality, which I want every man to read, I have a question I wish to answer: "Why am I, a man, writing on this topic?"

I have several reasons. After many years in my field, at least half the people I've counseled were women—from single to married, from homemaker to professional, from middle class to upper class, from high school dropout to doctoral degree. Many were sexually abused, many were not. Most were faithful to their husband, some were not. Almost all of them struggled sexually and relationally, and many grappled spiritually.

So many women I've counseled have been seriously hurt by a man. I'm deeply saddened, embarrassed, and angered by what some men do to women. Men can be so stupidly self-centered, and their actions are a spiritual injustice that contradicts the will of God.

I'll never forget the anger I felt years ago while counseling in New York City when a woman came to me with a serious marital problem and told me that when she sought the counsel of her pastor, he took advantage of her pain to seduce her. He was a prominent pastor in the city. May God have mercy, but I rest in the fact that vengeance belongs to God.

Another thing that angers me is that when men don't "get it" the damage is compounded and passes on to the next generation.

I began my counseling ministry believing that all women, while fallen, still possess an inner vision and understanding of biblically mature masculinity: they know a godly, mature man when they encounter one. Throughout my years of counseling I've grown in that conviction. Based on that premise I started my counseling career helping a sixteen-year-old girl deal with an incestuous relationship with her father, which had begun when she was only six years old. Many years later I counseled a twenty-six-year-old stripper who told me that from teen years to the present, she either was seduced by or had seduced every man she ever knew. In my heart and mind I had the same response to both these women and all others: I'm going to do everything I can, as God enables me, to show you mature, godly masculinity. Anything less is totally unacceptable, and God Himself will hold me accountable.

I also desire to speak the truth, not in the form of self-assertion, but to lead as a servant: not speaking on my own authority but as an advocate for the authority of Christ in women's lives, and not presuming my superiority or infallibility.

We correctly assume that a woman can show empathy, sympathy, understanding, and comfort to another woman. That is certainly true. Given the failure of many fathers and husbands, women may find too hard to believe that their husband can not only be that resource but also provide greater comfort. Another woman cannot offer the unique, benevolent love of strong, responsible, and mature masculinity. At one level, another woman can better understand another woman, and a man another man. However, I believe God has uniquely designed godly men to be able to offer resources not found in a female-to-female relationship. Just because men have sometimes miserably failed does not mean we should abandon what only a husband or male leadership can uniquely offer.

It should be obvious that women have a great deal to offer men, and men have a great deal to offer women. If that's not true, you would have to assume God didn't know what He was doing when He created both and put them in a marriage relationship. I relish the fact that I'm an older man writing these words. Being older doesn't mean I have it all together. However, I recognize some changes from my youth, such as where I am more caring and respectful, and pray that more and more as a mature man I am "sober-minded, dignified, self-controlled, sound in faith, in love and in steadfastness" (Titus 2:2). So I wish to communicate with older women as if to my mother, and to younger women as if to sisters and daughters.

Finally, you must know that I am not writing this chapter by myself. A woman of godly femininity has her hand in every word I write, a woman I have a deep love and appreciation for—Rosemary, my wife, best friend, lover, and God-given helper. Without her in my life, this book and my entire ministry of forty years would not exist. Through her I see the depth of wisdom God has given women. In nearly forty years of marriage, I have gained a growing appreciation of how God in His infinite wisdom created men and women equal, but so amazingly different. I see the equality and the differences, when lived out according to God's will, as being all to His glory.

God Designed Womanhood

"So God created man in his own image, in the image of God he created him; male and female he created them" (Genesis 1:27).

Several points need repeating in focusing attention on the design of womanhood. Sexuality is God's design for a woman. She is no less sexual than a man. Her body and her soul are designed to become one flesh with a man. All the physical nerve endings and sensory receptors are God-given to enjoy the intimacy and pleasure of sexual intercourse.

Mature men must grieve the sexual damage, sexual dysfunction, and sexual activity outside of marriage that mars the image of God in women. They must long to see sexual redemption brought to the hearts and minds of their sisters, wives, daughters, and friends.

Beyond sexuality we see more of the unique qualities of a woman that give us a clearer picture of God's design. As a female, she has the ability to bear children and fulfill God's command to reproduce. Women also have a high level of nurturing that is so clearly seen in motherhood. In addition, when focused clearly on the glory of God, there is an intuitiveness that serves the purpose of God and amazes godly men.

Everything a woman is (and a man too) images God. Sin significantly disrupts and seriously mars the image, but the likeness of God remains.[2] Is femininity an aspect of that image? Of course. And so is masculinity. God is neither male nor female, nor both. In *Recovering Biblical Manhood & Womanhood*, John Piper and Wayne Grudem write, "To say that our eyes image God, remember, is not to say that God has eyes; it is rather to say that our eyes picture something divine. Similarly, our sexuality pictures God's attributes and capacities."[3] To see God as either male or female distorts His divine, non-human nature.

In ways we can't fully comprehend, the image of God embraces everything female, everything male, and everything human. Therefore, I conclude that *the body of a godly woman should reinforce our perception of her imperishable beauty, and that her faith enhances the image of God and brings forth a gentleness, a quietness, and a feminine personality—all of which God sees and finds priceless* (see 1 Peter 3:4). In addition, genuine femininity also reveals courage and boldness! This is a woman who does not "fear anything that is frightening" (1 Peter 3:6). This is no stereotypical woman, but like the godly women of the Bible, she does good and trusts in God.

A Desire to Be Cherished

What is a woman's desire? Ask the question of any woman, single or married, and the answer is the same. Whether she is full of relational anticipation or a woman devastated by relational failure, both will know the answer intuitively: "I want to be cherished."

Cherished is the word that describes the longing of a woman's heart. You can define the word *cherished* with a dictionary, but you would run the risk of missing its personal, feminine meaning. In fact, for a woman, the word doesn't need to be defined. She knows in her heart exactly what it means to be cherished and knows instantly whether she is cherished or not. Only numbness, often resorted to in order to prevent pain, will limit the intuitive desire to be cherished. The desire, openly expressed from the heart, draws her to seek a Source that will not fail, that allows her to live, whether single or married, expressing unfading beauty to the world around her.

Being cherished is about the heart. We speak with our minds, but the warehouse of the heart determines the content of what we say. "For out of the overflow of the heart the mouth speaks. The good man brings good things out of the good stored up in him" (Matthew 12:34–35 NIV). When a woman is cherished by a man, she knows that the man has kept her fondly in mind. That is to say, she is the only one on his mind. The man's heart is a storehouse of good and delightful thoughts about his wife.

Ezekiel's wife was just such a woman. She is described as the delight of his eyes (Ezekiel 24:16). Imagine being the delight of your husband's eyes. Imagine even further that others in the community know that you are the delight of your husband's eyes.

This is not a matter of being pretty or sexy. Today, for so many women (and men) it is all about outward appearance; but looking good and being looked at don't get you what you want. The lustful look of a man fed by his deceitful heart, and a woman's attempt to be enticing, diminishes a woman's value, and she is not cherished.

A woman, with modesty and humility, can reveal an *unfading* beauty. Feminine beauty is intrinsically found in all women because they are the image of God and are made to be the image of God. True beauty never drags anyone into sin. Men should be able to notice in a woman the work of God, her femininity, with perfect naturalness and a godly heart.

Lori's story is heartbreaking. A young woman in her twenties and newly married, she was never the delight of her husband's eyes. Instead, he encouraged her to work as a stripper so that he could watch other men gawk at her. He exchanged the privilege and joy of an intimate, meaningful relationship with his wife for a despicable moment of false sensuality. This husband's heart, rather than good, was a staggering evil (see Matthew 12:35).

A Woman's Vulnerability

The need to be cherished is a position of vulnerability that is unpopular among many women today. Many feel that it is archaic and repressive that older women are to "train the younger women" in the blessings and context to be cherished, which is to "love their husbands, to be self-controlled, pure, working at home, kind, and submissive to their own husbands, that the word of God may not be reviled" (Titus 2:4–5). Instead, women are encouraged to live independent lives, to not wait around for a man to cherish them. Wouldn't that be codependent? The message preached is, "Take care of yourself, because most likely no one else will."

I think God likes it when we show our trust in Him by our dependence. He longs for us to be vulnerable, first with Him, then—having a goal and purpose in God—with each other.

We prefer to think it's okay to *want*, but we hate the prospect of being *needy*. There is a negative connotation to the word that suggests a picture of a weak, pathetic woman who is deemed unworthy of affection. Increasingly, some women don't like to see themselves as being in need, especially in need of a man. A self-sufficient woman is admired. Her independence is a virtue. The fact that she is able to make it on her own is a sign of a true woman.

However, the desire is there, it's unavoidable, and the inherent desire leads in only one direction—toward the need for relationship, specifically, a covenant relationship with a man.

No question, the risk of desire is substantial, so substitutes abound—put all the focus on children, overspend on credit cards, overeat, or lose yourself in the fantasy of a romance novel. From the very first moment that a girl starts noticing boys, the tension begins. Fear increases when she is the only one not going to the school prom. Things get progressively worse in her senior year of college when all her friends have married or are engaged to be married. She runs in fear from the sense of need and prefers to only touch the surface of what she wants.

She may even hook up with a guy just to fill the void. The desire is forever, and so is the uncertainty. The internal battle rages on with a cloud of fear enveloping the soul, driven by the question, "Will anyone ever really love and cherish *me*?"

Sexual redemption becomes a reality when the imperishable beauty of longing to be cherished finds itself in pursuit of the will of God. Feminine desire has a beauty all its own because God invented it.

Who Will Rule?

How we as sinful men and women express control differs. Through our original corruption coming from Adam, the masculine expression is to be silent and to listen to his wife rather than to God and to not express decisive leadership.

The feminine expression of control revolves around authority. She turns from godly authority, listens to the authority of an enemy, wants to have more authority in being like God, seeks more authority by desiring to become wise (see Genesis 3:6), and then ignores authority by leading her husband to do the same thing. Defying the authority of God is the ultimate issue in all rebellion and in all sin.

The sexual and relational symptoms of sin for women include a great emphasis on body image and appearance, becoming immodest, having less sexual interest in marriage, being more controlling relationally, embracing certain aspects of feminism, demonstrating unfaithfulness, and choosing serial monogamy.[4]

God's judgment for women in Genesis 3:16 involves physical pain in childbirth and relational pain in marriage. "I will surely multiply your pain in childbearing; in pain you shall bring forth children. Your desire shall be for your husband and he shall rule over you." The pain comes in her conflict with her husband and/or in his domination of his wife. The relational pain can be seen in two ways. Several commentaries point to a similarity between *desire* in Genesis 3:16 and *desire* in Genesis 4:7: "Its [sin's] *desire* is for you, but you must rule over it." In other words, sin has the desire to control each of us, and it often does through the wickedness, deceitfulness, and arrogance of our own hearts. Temptations come from within, from our sinful inclinations, and from external objects as well. That is why the offer of a cyber relationship through your computer's Internet access is first an internal temptation, then an external temptation. Many people have no problem sitting alone at their computer with full Internet access, without a filter or accountability software, and are not tempted. Many other people can't resist. The explanation is *not* an addiction or disease rooted in your family of origin, but an inward desire for selfish fulfillment.

As sin desires to control us, a woman's desire is to control her husband. On the issue of who's in charge of the marriage and family, there are women who control passively and others aggressively. Some women deny their femininity by living as a doormat. Some passive women don't look like it, but they are very controlling, and often get what they want by manipulation.

You have rule on one hand and subjection (with a desire to control) on the other—both of which are the result of the fall. The resulting conflict is going to directly impact love, sex, and and all other aspects of the relationship. In other words, how a man and a woman in marriage handle rule and subjection in a fallen world will show itself relationally and sexually. The woman desires her husband, in the sense that sin desires control in our lives (Genesis 4:7). The judgment of God is not that a woman will now have a sexual and relational desire for her husband—both desires already existed before the fall, and were good. But the man, as part of the curse of the fall, will control. (Note that this is a separate issue from the headship/leadership that God ordained for Adam.) Control can take two forms: one is to dictate what we want and expect the other person to respond, while the other is to control our own pain or rejection when others fail to give us what we want.

As sinners, everyone is a controlling person—we just have different styles. Control in fallen relationships is a complex, deeply tangled web where often the dominant person feels controlled by the passive person (covertly controlling). The passive person always feels controlled by domination, but is nevertheless controlling themselves. In other words, each person, whether dominant or passive, is controlling and being controlled. A husband can choose to be a wimp, but is still controlling the impact of the relationship on himself. Or, he can be a controlling tyrant. Sexually, the wimp in his attempt to control may be impotent or lack sexual interest. The woman can control by being a doormat while the man never gets what he wants sexually or relationally, and she feels like a sexual object. On the other hand, she can be a usurper and never get what she wants. She may lack sexual interest or feel power in being sexy. Either way, controlling relational desires passively or dominantly is a relational nightmare.

Every woman I have talked with in counseling wants a more meaningful relationship with her husband. I think all women, my wife included, want this, even if a man is a wimp. But when you try to get your husband to respond more meaningfully—sexually, relationally, and spiritually, what do you get in return? *He still rules!* He decides if he wants to respond or not. If he doesn't want to, he's not going to. He shuts down, pulls away. You could have more success in trying to get a mountain to move. A mature, godly husband, on the other hand, will reverse course and respond in "an understanding way, showing honor to the woman as the weaker vessel" (1 Peter 3:7). But the fact remains—the passive wimp sexually and relationally runs away while the woman dominates every decision. She doesn't get what she is longing for but, on the other hand, she assumes control and moves things in the direction she wants. The man doesn't feel like he is in control in his passivity, but in reality, by blocking her feminine desire he strongly controls by saying under his breath, "You're not getting anything from me, woman!"

The desire for control operates on two levels of conflict: The first concerns who is going to run the marriage. This is a headship or leadership issue. Second, control is about getting what you want relationally. If you handle the first badly, the second is immediately impacted. In other words, as women attempt to get what they want, there is often a strong element of controlling. In response, men irresponsibly back off and leadership diminishes. In pulling away, relational masculinity deteriorates and the relationship a woman wants is lost and/or she is left feeling like a sexual object when approached physically.

We often think that the controlling person is outspoken, confrontational, or dictatorial, but some of the most controlling people are quiet, unassuming, and very passive. I learned this the hard way in graduate school when my psychology professor correctly observed that I was not saying a word in my small group. As a professor of psychology, I thought he would be understanding and empathic when I explained that I was intimidated by the other members of the group and felt like I had little or nothing to share that was worthwhile. His response seemed incorrect and insensitive when he said, "You're freaking everybody out!" He meant that I was controlling the group, which made no sense to me. Next week in small group I sat quietly without saying a word, but kept hearing him say, "You're freaking everybody out!" Then I noticed that before everyone else shared and after they shared they looked at me. They were trying to read my response. Then it hit me: "I'm freaking everyone out!" I was controlling the group dynamic and the group's effectiveness.

Seeking to satisfy relational desire by controlling the other person is a relational nightmare. Several years ago I counseled a pastor of a small struggling church who was paid only a meager salary. He was the biggest wimp I have ever met. As just mentioned, the more a man wimps out, the more a wife rules the roost. He admitted avoiding decisions in the marriage. His wife was one of the most dominant women I've ever seen in counseling. She admitted that she had consciously married the weakest man she could find so he would never dominate her. Foolishly, she had achieved the control she wanted, but had lost out sexually and relationally. She never asked for intimacy. He found satisfaction elsewhere. Secretly, he had amassed over fifty thousand dollars in credit card debt spent on prostitutes.

All attempts to sinfully control relationally and sexually lead to more relational pain and chaos. Meaningful sex and relationship will come only when both the husband and wife are in subjection to the order and commands of God for His glory.

Foolishness abounds. Women blame men; men blame women. But the fact is, God in His judgment at the beginning of time and in His providence allows pain to come out of our experience of life. At the very beginning of time, Adam and Eve stepped out from under God's authority in an attempt to enhance their lives. Their rebellion led to God's judgment for both of them—pain, frustration, and futility. To this day we seek to avoid the reality of God's judgment. We choose a different path to deal with the profound disorder of all of life. The arrogance in us all that attempts to get control over all the difficult circumstances of life by our own efforts is a foolish attempt to question or replace a sovereign God. Oswald Chambers wrote in *My Utmost for His Highest*, "The nature of sin is not immorality and wrongdoing, but the nature of self-realization which leads us to say, 'I am my own god.'"[5]

The Unavoidable Reality

There is no escape from the reality of the fall. Sexually and relationally, the fall is as real as the discomfort we experience in being emotionally naked and confused with an enduring sense of shame.

Universally, all the assurances of relational happiness succumb to a never-ending cycle of gain and loss when the honeymoon is over. The heart knows that relationship is not meaningless, but is frustrated in its efforts to find consistent fulfillment. This is your life. This is my life. This is everyone's life. The reality of disappointment resulting from our separation from God permeates all of life. It extends well beyond relationships. Work feels more satisfying in a bull market, a flourishing career, a consistent paycheck, and the potential for advancement. Yet underneath it all is a strong undertow that can pull us under faster than we can swim. Even if we elude financial failure, "He who loves money will not be satisfied with money, nor he who loves wealth with his income; this also is vanity" (Ecclesiastes 5:10). The only true hope for satisfaction is to stop living our way and start living God's way.

Many would agree that there is a secret struggle to what some falsely define as "becoming a woman." In the shadows, women have shifted from frequent petting without intercourse to frequent intercourse without petting. The pride in one's body secretly becomes an illicit pleasure from immodesty. The authentic desire to be cherished is replaced by a substitute desire for sexual attention—finding sex in all the wrong places. The problem is that a natural desire is turned into an evil desire on the inside, both for the man looking with lustful intent and the woman wanting to look sexy for men. Desire will control you, or you will control the desire (see James 1:14–15). This desire for attention may also lead to wanting it from another woman.

The danger is that the natural desire to be cherished can easily and quickly turn into a distorted desire for male attention, whether emotional or physical. Caught in deception, a woman will publicly still cling to a sexually pure image while concealing a sexual fantasy or a sexual encounter. Dishonesty preserves the dream of looking good on the outside by adamantly saying, "I've never done that before; that's not me."

A Christian woman with adult married children, after a two-year affair with a colleague at work, said to me, "I don't know what got into me; I despise adultery."

Sexual redemption begins when God shows us the deceitfulness of our own hearts. What follows from that revelation is real change for the glory of God.

Sexual redemption is all about hope! But before we can embrace redemption, we must face another sobering reality.

The Path to Sexual Redemption

1 Have you ever felt cherished? Have you ever felt cherished enough?

2 When you feel your husband doesn't pay enough attention to you, what's your response?

3 When you feel neglected, do you shop and spend money, or overeat, to fill the soul? Do you look for attention from another man and justify fantasy, immodesty, flirting, cybersex, or hooking up?

4 As John Piper has pointed out in numerous places and times, "God is most glorified in us when we are most satisfied in him." The core problem of the human heart is not that our desires are too strong, but rather they are too weak! Are you seeing the weakness of your own desires and are you ready for a life that is more deeply satisfying?

CHAPTER EIGHT

The Real Problem

I carry about with me an evil heart,
I know that without thee I can do nothing,
that everything with which I shall be concerned,
however harmless in itself,
may prove an occasion of sin or folly,
unless I am kept by thy power.[1]

As my initial meeting with Jim and Carrie continued, Carrie told her side of the story. The ugliness of Jim's sin and the damage done to his wife made the pain palpable in the room.

I asked Carrie, "Do you want to say more? What else are you feeling about all this?"

"I am so angry! I don't know who I should tell about this and who I shouldn't! It's embarrassing—we are, were, known as having one of the best marriages in our church! I had to go talk to the pastor and ask him if I should kick Jim out. I did, you know! And I can't pray or sleep or hardly eat. I'm depressed. What should I tell the kids? They are all gone now, but I talk to them every few days. My sons knew something was wrong, so I finally told them too. Our daughter, Susan, got really mad and told me I should divorce him because he had lied to me all these years. She started screaming too on the phone. It was terrible."

Carrie paused for another drink of water, then continued, "I hate this,

Dr. Schaumburg. I'm humiliated. And I don't know if I want this marriage to continue. I don't know how I could ever trust him again."

She stopped briefly and wept, her shoulders shaking. "Why does he have to look at that trash when I'm more than willing to have sex with him? I can't compete with all that! But he doesn't hardly want to touch me! What's so awful about me? When we did have sex, it was like he wasn't really there. He was always trying to maneuver me and make little suggestions. Now I know what was going on! He was thinking about his porn. I hate what he was thinking about. Why couldn't he just love me? I don't get it! I don't want him to touch me . . . I don't want to be here, really. Do I want to stay married to him? I don't know . . ."

Jim slumped in his chair and stared straight ahead. His expression was blank, but I sensed anger and shame rumbling inside of him. He did not speak.

I never watch horror films. The idea of suddenly being scared out of my seat by some heinous, diabolical creature bent on everyone's destruction is not my idea of entertainment. Yet the human heart in all its deceitfulness is scarier.

The countless stories—like Jim and Carrie's—I have heard of the horror of sexual sin, unfaithfulness, and sexual brokenness could fill volumes. However, hearing so much about the darker side of sexual activity, coupled with consistent study of Scripture, has led me to a stronger belief in our total depravity, the unmerited grace of God, and imputed righteousness.

In dealing with sinful sexuality, pornography is the pervading problem for most folk. Adultery, both in affairs and impersonal sex, would be a close second. These are followed by everything else that's in the secret shadows: prostitution, child molestation, homosexuality, lap dances, massage parlors, cross-dressing, and fetishes and adult babies (adults who wear diapers in public and urinate or defecate for sexual arousal). Over the years I have seen the awfulness, commonness, and filthiness of secret sexual sin exposed in the lives of pastors, missionaries, and ordinary people in Christ's church. I know this: no amount of graduate or postgraduate training or professional certification and licensure can prepare you to deal with the messy sin in people's lives. And the problems have a common source—the heart.

Heart Problem

We cannot afford to soft-pedal, overlook, or ignore what's on the inside of all of us. When we do, we only see sin's pains and disasters. We grab up books on self-help and "how-to" guides to change our difficult situation. Seduced by human techniques, we attempt to superficially heal ourselves and others, forgetting that "out of the heart come evil thoughts, murder, adultery, sexual immorality, theft, false witness, slander. These are what defile a person" (Matthew 15:19–20).

Some popular authors and speakers passionately declare that believers, because of their standing in Christ, have good hearts. Others reduce the existence of sin in someone's life to Satan's influence or otherwise avoid the issues of an impure heart and choose to deal primarily with family dysfunctions, personal trauma, an addictive society, worthlessness, loneliness, denial, blame-shifting, codependency, shame and guilt, and human need. Sinclair Ferguson is not one of those authors. He writes, "Jesus speaks about adultery, but it is clear from his exposition that he has *any* sexual immorality in view. He stresses that its root is to be found in the heart. The man who *looks* at a woman *lustfully* commits heart adultery with her."[2]

What's on the inside is worse than anything we hear in someone's words or actions. In fact, you can never describe what's on the inside of my heart and your heart. If we could see each other at that level, we would run in terror. What amazing grace that God would reach out to such wretches.

Sin is not a little "goof up" or "innocent mistake." The seriousness of sin will not be fully understood when a spouse only feels the pain he or she has inflicted. All sin is an attack on God and dishonors Him. All forms of unfaithfulness are first against God, then a spouse. "Against you, you only, have I sinned and done what is evil in your sight" (Psalm 51:4).

Sinners are referred to by Jesus Christ as "workers of lawlessness" (Matthew 7:23). Sexual sinners are lawbreakers. This is not a simple speeding ticket on the path of life, but instead an armed robbery, a serious felony charge in the court of heaven. There is no third-degree unfaithfulness, nor second-degree adultery. There are no reduced sentences or plea-bargaining to a lesser crime. There is only one degree of sexual sin against God, and the required penalty under the law that must be upheld is death.

Someone will say, "Harry, that is shaming; a guilt trip. You are a dangerous man!" It has been reported to me on several occasions that counselors have told a person I later counseled, "Don't go to Schaumburg for help, don't read his book *False Intimacy*, because he is dangerous. He actually believes there is something wrong with people who sexually sin."

Yes, I do believe that! And I strongly believe there is something drastically wrong with me and everyone around me. My point is, you can't minimize sin, especially sexual sin. Sinclair Ferguson writes, "The lust that leads to adultery will also lead a man to hell. Better to deal with the lust now—to deny oneself now—than to live with eternal self-recrimination. Far from simply forbidding *some* acts of immorality, Jesus says God's law demands purity and integrity in our hearts and in our thoughts about others. Sexual relations have become the door through which many professing Christian have walked to their destruction."[3]

None of us can boast: Whatever godliness we possess is a result of God's work in our heart. We all have the same heart past and heart potential. "For we ourselves were once foolish, disobedient, led astray, slaves to various passions and pleasures, passing our days in malice and envy, hated by others and hating one another" (Titus 3:3).

If we are innocent of sexual sin, we are tempted to call it purity. We look at sexual sin in others, including a spouse, and ask preposterous questions: "How could you?" "What were you thinking?" These are questions asked by a person who has not come to grips with the awfulness in their own heart.

Without a proper and penetrating understanding of grace and sin, we will be unprepared to deal with the horrible nature of sexual sin and the brokenness of sexuality all around us. The depravity of the heart and the inborn evil of the soul is real. When we fully grasp our innate condition, we are greatly humbled by "Jesus Christ, who became to us . . . our righteousness and sanctification and redemption" (1 Corinthians 1:30). Once we are in Christ, we realize we can have no confidence in our own "righteousness," but are totally dependent on "that which comes through faith in Christ, the righteousness from God that depends on faith" (Philippians 3:9). Practically speaking, this *imputed* righteousness becomes the foundation for *imparted* righteousness. First, because we stand condemned, Christ provides *justification* by which we are instantaneously made righteous; thus we now stand before God not "guilty" but "righteous" in His sight. This is *imputed* righteousness. Second, because we live in bondage to sexual sin by our natural, internal disposition, the Holy Spirit works in our lives to purify our thoughts and deeds. This is *imparted* righteousness. If we embrace this great work of grace, our hearts are transformed and we cannot live in a pattern of habitual sin. Such believers are not perfect, but you "will recognize them by their fruits" (Matthew 7:16).

What Is Sin?

Scripture uses a wide variety of terms to describe sin. Sin is unbelief, rebellion, and perversion. A common thread characterizing sin is the failure to fulfill the law of God. Sin is not conforming to the requirements of God, and includes our inward thoughts and motives. Sin involves actions and motives, but it also includes an inner disposition or state.

After dealing with so much sexual sin in people's lives, I like this definition: *Sin is a failure to let God be God.* Ultimately, sin results from placing ourselves and our desires ahead of God.

Putting God first is the first of the Ten Commandments in the Old Testament. In the New Testament Jesus reiterates this primary commandment: "And you shall love the Lord your God with all your heart and with all your soul and with all your mind and with all your strength" (Mark 12:30). That is why idolatry is the essence of sin. If we seek our own will and what we want to do, we seek what satisfies us before we seek God; we first seek out what feeds our well-being—and we can end up seeking spirituality above seeking God and His will. Thus we end up placing our values above God Himself. And the result is that God is not God in our hearts! It is not "my utmost for His highest;" it is "my utmost for myself."

What leads to and causes sin? We must answer this question with complete accuracy because it directly affects the elimination of sin. Be aware that in our therapeutic culture sin is often psychologized as a symptom of woundedness or caused by woundedness. To teach that wickedness is a real problem is seen as negative and destructive to a person's self-esteem. However, if sin is caused by wickedness and corruption, the cure of sin is not a superficial technique leading to behavior management, feeling anger toward your parents, or diverting your eyes.

The ultimate cause of sin is an evil heart. We are born spiritually corrupt. We are dead! "And you were dead in the trespasses and sins . . . carrying out the desires of the body and the mind, and were by nature children of wrath, like the rest of mankind" (Ephesians 2:1, 3). We need a new nature, a new heart. Like using a household hammer instead of a jackhammer to break up concrete, behavior-altering techniques are the wrong tools for the job. What is needed is a supernatural transformation, and sexual redemption is part of that transformation.

Grace AND Works

The warnings in the New Testament against persistent sexual sin raise an extremely important question. John Piper asks it this way: "How do we enjoy security in Jesus when what he requires is real change of heart and real righteous behavior?"[4] I fully agree with Piper's answer, even if it is the minority view. "Think of our sense of security—our assurance that we are going to enter the final manifestation of the kingdom of God at the end of the age—resting most decisively on our *location* in God's invincible favor, but also on our behavioral *demonstration* that we are truly in that location."[5] Piper goes on to clarify "demonstration":

> What I mean by the *demonstration* is that the way we live shows our location. It does not create the location. God establishes our location through faith alone. But he has ordained that it be fitting for the location to have a demonstration in the world. This is the righteousness that exceeds that of the scribes and Pharisees. It is necessary, not optional.[6]

How does this apply to the look that Jesus called "lustful intent"? Piper again gives wonderful clarity, and I fully relate to his experience and grave concern.

> I have learned again and again from firsthand experience that there are many professing Christians who have a view of salvation that disconnects it from the real life, and that nullifies the threats of the Bible, and puts the sinning person who claims to be a Christian beyond the reach of biblical warnings. I believe this view of the Christian life is comforting thousands who are on the broad way that leads to destruction (Matthew 7:13). Jesus said, if you don't fight lust, you won't go to heaven. Not that saints always succeed. The issue is that we resolve to fight, not that we succeed flawlessly.[7]

Is this not contrary to the thinking and teaching of our day? Many would say, by the way they live, "If I have grace, His unconditional love, I don't have to put a lot of effort into holiness or obedience." Larry was a pastor who frequently looked at pornography. His wife was devastated when she found pornography on his laptop. In counseling he said, "I know it's wrong,

I know that it bothers Cindy, and I'd like to stop, but God loves me anyway." Yes, He does! God is also displeased and requires obedience from His children. The exhortation is clear: Given that we "have been raised with Christ" (Colossians 3:1) and "have died, and your life is hidden with Christ" (Colossians 3:3), "put to death therefore what is earthly in you: sexual immorality, impurity, passion, evil desire, and covetousness, which is idolatry. On account of these the wrath of God is coming" (Colossians 3:5–6). "But now you must put them all away: anger, wrath, malice, slander, and obscene talk from your mouth" (Colossians 3:8). On top of all that deliberate "putting away," we must "put on" (see Colossians 3:12–17) a lot more.

Why should we be concerned with holiness, including sexual purity, since we are saved by grace? This is not a new question. John Calvin forcefully answered: "What is proclaimed concerning the mercy of God is seized by some as an occasion of licentiousness; while others are hindered by slothfulness from meditating on 'newness of life.' But the manifestation of the grace of God unavoidably carries along with it exhortation to a holy life."[8]

A divided heart produces desires that must be brought under control or denied. If we are hell bent on committing spiritual suicide—as we are in our fallen state—our response to sin must be fierce. If sin is an active pattern, the diagnosis is unquestionable. Let's go deeper in our understanding of sin by reflecting on a sermon Charles Spurgeon preached in 1883. His text was 1 John 3:8: "Whoever makes a practice of sinning is of the devil, for the devil has been sinning from the beginning. The reason the Son of God appeared was to destroy the works of the devil." Spurgeon points out that the "works of the devil" is descriptive of sin and John is saying that Christ came to destroy those works—that is, sin. We shun the thought that our sins are so corrupt in God's view that all sin could be said to be the "works of the devil." Rather than avoiding this disturbing description, let us embrace it, as Spurgeon suggests: "Oh, if men could but see the slime of the serpent upon their pleasurable sins, the venom of asps upon their dainty lusts, and the smoke of hell upon their proud and boastful thoughts, surely they would loathe that which they now delight in. If sin connects us with the devil himself, let us flee from it as from a devouring lion. The expression [sin as the works of the devil] is a word of detestation: may it enter into our hearts and make sin horrible to us."[9]

In Matthew 5:29–30 Jesus said, "If your right eye causes you to sin, tear it out and throw it away. For it is better that you lose one of your members than that your whole body be thrown into hell." Commenting on this passage, John Piper writes: "When dealing with the impurity of inward sexual lust, Jesus demands whatever it takes to defeat it because our souls are at stake."[10]

Receiving Grace

If we believe the teaching of Jesus Christ about our hearts, then we will quickly open the door of grace with decisive repentance. Grace is the hope of real change. Everyone with a sexual sin problem has struggled to stop. With perhaps decades of failed attempts, discouragement is real. The wife of a man who can't stop looking at pornography has either given up hope or long ago abandoned the marriage, even if she still lives with her husband. I'm convinced that without the grace of God, real change is impossible. First, we must see sin as sin, then have God reveal to us at a heart level His amazing grace.

I have seen it in the eyes and heard it in the words of hundreds upon hundreds of spouses. The tragedy of unfaithfulness is painfully real. In almost every case the unfaithful wither in shame and self-pity. But there is nothing in that whole experience that necessarily leads to conviction of sin. Oswald Chambers wrote, "The conviction of sin is one of the most uncommon things that ever happens to a person. It is the beginning of an understanding of God."[11]

Conviction is a deep spiritual sorrow for sin. It is not disgust or the shame of being caught. True conviction is founded on convincing evidence of our wickedness and that God has good reason for having placed us under His wrath. Conviction is the full persuasion of the truth of God, found in the gospel, of our unholy condition and God's holy state.

In seeing God's glory we are humbled to the dust. For the depraved heart, full of original corruption, it is impossible on our own to achieve conviction that leads to repentance of sin. God's mercy and grace are His initiative, not ours. We are too corrupt to even want real change. Based on sound biblical doctrine, we understand that in our struggle with sin, divine illumination and persuasion are required for the heart so deceived to respond.[12] True conviction is an indication that God is at work, and with godly sorrow comes the power to seek real change—a change of heart.

In the New Testament, the phrase "the grace of God" is used to describe God's unmerited favor. Grace is God's love for us undeserving sinners with deceitful, wicked hearts; God's unmerited favor active in those same hearts; and the dynamic of the Holy Spirit's transformation of the evil heart. Grace is never passive but penetrates the darkness for God's divine purpose and glory. There is so much of God's work we cannot see.

The unmerited grace of God, that is in Christ Jesus, is extended to all types of people, regardless of what they have done, from sweet little old grandmothers to prostitutes with a brazen look; from a sexually pure spouse to a husband living as a sexual predator seducing hundreds of women for his own pleasure; from a loving, devoted father to the self-centered wretch of a man who steals his daughter's virginity; from a woman with unfading beauty to the immodest woman intent on drawing attention to her body; to the couple enjoying meaningful intimacy for the glory of God to the couple lost in the foolishness of false intimacy in their own marriage; and from the couple who are virgins on their wedding night to the unmarried couple full of uncontrolled passion who find no delight in sexual purity.

The grace of God brings redemption to *all* who are called (see 2 Thessalonians 2:13–14; 2 Timothy 1:9–10). It imputes a righteousness that is not our own; nothing that we have earned. This grace motivates not from self-disgust, self-contempt, or contempt from others, but brings us to a place where we are intolerant of the evil in ourselves. "For the grace of God that brings salvation. . . . teaches us to say 'No' to ungodliness and worldly passions" (Titus 2:11–12 NIV). The recovery community says that you can't "Just say no!" to sexual addiction. The problem with their understanding is what the word *just* implies. The true believer isn't saying "no" alone. The whole grace of God stands behind him also saying "no!" Knowing the grace of God is a "no" with faith in the power of God's work and for the purpose of His glory. The true believer is *never* powerless regarding the problem in his heart. The grace of God breaks the back of uncontrolled sexual desires and is the only antidote for sexual sin.

The key biblical truth of this chapter is that our original corruption, which infuses every human heart, makes us incapable of obeying God (see 1 Corinthians 2:14–15). The frustration in making real change is the heart and mind butting up against this reality. Sin is a bondage that has no human rescue plan. This is humbling to the independent, take-charge attitude of our day. We must realize that this corruption makes it impossible to believe the truth of the gospel on our own. As you read this chapter, you may feel frustration and hopelessness. But the good news, and it is very good news, is that "while we were still weak, at the right time Christ died for the ungodly" and "God showed his love for us in that while we were still sinners, Christ died for us" (Romans 5:6–8).

So then, because of the work of Christ alone, we now have a "measure of freedom."[13] Jesus taught, "Truly, truly, I say to you, everyone who commits sin is a slave to sin." But this is our hope: "If the Son sets you free, you will be free indeed" (John 8:34, 36). We must first understand the bondage; then we can understand the freedom. True freedom is to serve God and to fulfill His purpose—which is only possible by the grace of God. Yet the freedom that God gives in redemption requires our active response. As the heart experiences real change, we come to understand Robert Peterson's observation that "Scripture affirms divine sovereignty, and at the same time teaches that there is human freedom in the sense of genuine human responsibility to God. We can understand much of the relationship between them, but mystery remains."[14]

First Things First: Repent

In a word, the teaching of Jesus is, "Unless you repent, you will all likewise perish" (Luke 13:3). John Piper writes in *What Jesus Demands from the World*, "The first demand of Jesus' public ministry was 'Repent.' He spoke this command indiscriminately to all who would listen. It was a call for radical *inward* change toward God and man."[15]

Repentance is what happens on the inside; it is not an effort to change behavior through a process of steps or choosing to look away when tempted to lust. The exhortation of Jesus is to "Bear fruits in keeping with repentance" (Luke 3:8). A change of heart on the inside changes our sexuality on the outside. It bears fruit of sexual purity, faithfulness, modesty, and God-glorifying sexual intimacy between one man and one woman.

Repentance also involves a change of authority, an adjustment in who rules. "Repent, for the kingdom of heaven is at hand" (Matthew 4:17). Prior to repentance, we rule ourselves; after repentance, God rules. If we are a true believer, the reign of God has already started. The Lord Himself is ruling more and more in our heart. The message of the kingdom and the rule of the kingdom give us a vision of a new lifestyle of sexual purity, purpose in our sexuality, and change in our relationship with others. But how will we get there?

We are in bondage to sin and therefore it takes divine illumination and persuasion for the heart to respond. This is a very old and fundamental concept stated even in Jeremiah's day: "Can the Ethiopian change his skin or the leopard its spots? Neither can you do good who are accustomed to doing evil" (Jeremiah 13:23 NIV). We are so corrupt, enslaved to sexual sin, that repentance is impossible apart from God's illumination. If your heart is open to pay attention to the truth, you are blessed!

Sexually, what we are up against is our own stubborn nature. The following list illustrates the heart's deceitfulness in the area of sexual sin:

- The sexual sinner always acts like he or she is sexually pure
- The sexual sinner always justifies the sexual sin
- The sexual sinner always declares that sexual sin is a need
- The sexual sinner always deceives himself or herself into believing that sinning sexually will be a positive benefit
- The sexual sinner always makes excuses for his or her sexual sin
- The sinner who does not sexually sin tells himself or herself that his or her heart is good

Is there anything that we excuse or justify in ourselves or others that is poisoning our hearts and minds or the lives of others? If you answered "no," before you move on too quickly, I encourage you to search the Scriptures. The exhortation is clear: "Examine yourselves, to see whether you are in the faith. Test yourselves. Or do you not realize this about yourselves, that Jesus Christ is in you?—unless indeed you fail to meet the test" (2 Corinthians 13:5). The threat of deception is real and it requires us to ask honest questions about our own sexuality.

Illumination begins the process of salvation, and is a continual work of God throughout our life's journey. Simply put, we are far too corrupt on our own to change our hearts and show the fruit of repentance. At the same time, we are commanded to change. Repentance is not a one-time action; it takes place every day in the life of a true believer. Paul wrote, "Do you presume on the riches of his kindness and forbearance and patience, not knowing that God's kindness is meant to lead you to repentance?" (Romans 2:4).

The situation is desperate.

But help has arrived!

The Path to Sexual Redemption

1 Why is the sin of unfaithfulness more serious than the relational devastation it causes?

2 Why are we completely dependent on God's gracious intervention?

3 Why do you think both grace and works (obedience) are critical in your life?

4 You may have repented of your past sexual sin, but are you continually repentant over the imperfection of other areas of your life (see 1 John 1:9)?

CHAPTER NINE

The Change That Brings Freedom

Take away my roving eye, curious ear, greedy
appetite, lustful heart;
show me that none of these things
can heal a wounded conscience,
or support a tottering frame,
or uphold a departing spirit,
then take me to the cross and leave me there.[1]

As Carrie gave her blow-by-blow summary of Jim's sexual unfaithfulness, Jim seemed to visibly shrink in his chair. Was this evidence of true repentance or just a way of revealing his regret and shame? Time would tell.

"I know this is terribly painful," I said to Carrie. Then I addressed her husband: "Jim, when you see Carrie hurting like this, what does that stir in you?"

"I can't believe I've done this and hurt her so bad. My daughter doesn't want to talk to me. I'm mad at myself. Maybe I have an addiction? I've read a couple of books, and I can't seem to win over this—I could be a sex addict."

"Do you think he's a sex addict?" Carrie interrupted. "Is there any hope for this? Is this treatment going to work?"

"Yes, there is a lot of hope," I answered. "You are in the right place. I urge you both to stay in the process, though. Do the assignments scheduled for today and tomorrow. Don't fight with each other, okay? Give each other some space. Do all the work—the homework and reading. Go for walks. Ask the Holy Spirit to reveal what's really the state of your heart. Look beyond your problems and pain to the root causes. Plead with God to reveal sins that may be hidden. I'll see you again in a couple of days. If you need to talk to me in the meantime, let me know."

With that we stood and said our temporary good-byes.

Sexual sin is enslavement to sexual activity, a state of mind, a self-centeredness that pushes away the truth. Even the negative consequences of sexual sin do not produce change because they lack the ability to effect repentance. In this chapter let's look at what is required for sexual redemption—heart change that is real and lasting.

True Repentance Means Change

Repentance is the grace of God at work inwardly where the sinner is not only made humble but visibly changed. We don't see the sin that is on the inside, we only see the behavior. We must be willing to go beyond saying, "I have sinned!" Repentance states what the sin actually is and that we no longer want that sin in our heart and life.

In repentance we move from our self-centered will to a desire for the will of God *alone* in the context of a particular behavioral sin. Self must die. God must reign.

I have sat with many men who have lost a ministry, a career, and/or a marriage as they wept and wrung their hands, knowing they had thrown everything away; but I could tell there was little agony of soul. The greatest loss is the favor of God's pleasure in His purchased slave. Bought with a great price, the sexual sinner, who should be a slave of righteousness, has returned to the pig pen of slavery to sin that dishonors his Master. It's not a pretty sight.

Here's what genuine repentance would sound like as a husband speaks to his wife: "I sinned and committed adultery with Susan, your best friend. I have sinned against God. I want to follow the will of God, not sinning against you and the children. I want to live a holy life before God by being a faithful husband and devoted father as God enables me."

The sexual sinner finds satisfaction not only in sexual pleasure, but also, ironically, through an illusory control of personal desires that arranges life on their terms. Repentance changes all that and sends the sexual sinner in a new direction.

Thomas Watson lists six specific elements that are necessary for repentance:[2]

- **Sight of Sin.** Sin must be seen for what it is, a deadly plague of the heart. This insight must humble the person
- **Sorrow for Sin.** "The sacrifices of God are a broken spirit; a broken and contrite heart, O God, you will not despise" (Psalm 51:17). God works to create heartfelt repentance and obedience, not just outward behavioral change
- **Confession of Sin.** In confrontation, a person is accused of sexual sin. In confession, the sexual sinner is self-accusing. In confession there is a deep resentment for one's sin
- **Shame of Sin.** "That which would make us blush is that *the sins we commit are far worse than the sins of the heathen.* We acted against more light. . . . The Christian sins against clearer conviction"[3]
- **Hatred of Sin.** "How far are they from repentance who, instead of hating sin, love sin! To the godly sin is a thorn in the eye; to the wicked it is as a crown on the head: 'When thou doest evil, then thou rejoicest' (Jeremiah 11:15 KJV). Loving of sin is worse than committing it"[4]
- **Turning from Sin**. "True sorrow for sin is *eminently practical.* No man can say he hates sin if he lives in it. Repentance makes us see the evil of sin not merely as a theory but experimentally [experientially]—as a burn victim dreads fire"[5]

Heart change is highly motivated change. This is not the motivation of self-disgust or sadness about the harm done to others. It is a higher calling.

Scripture Fuels Authentic Change

Dr. Gregory Laughery, who lives and teaches at the L'Abri Fellowship community in Switzerland, states, "The need for Scripture as our map becomes clear as we reflect upon the two-fold challenge facing us: the rising attraction to cultural and non-Christian forms of spirituality on the one hand, and the impoverishment of Christian spirituality on the other."[6]

Laughery goes on to rightly insist on sound doctrine and scriptural teaching to avoid self-deception where we "end up following what we assume the path should be, although this assumption can in fact be leading us in the wrong direction."[7] In contrast, following Scripture means we seek "*its* direction, *its* lighting, *its* perspectives and then how these apply to illuminating the path ahead of us."[8] Hebrews 4:12 reveals the power of God's Word: "For the word of God is living and active, sharper than any two-edged sword, piercing to the division of soul and of spirit, of joints and of marrow, and discerning the thoughts and intentions of the heart."

The Bible is not a normal book whose authority depends on the insights of the human writers. The Bible has authority because of the credibility of the Author—God. Since it is the only written revelation of God, the Bible is to direct our beliefs and behaviors.

The Scriptures are sufficient, containing everything we need to know to attain deliverance from sexual sin, as well as salvation and eternal life. It is not a book on sex or marriage, but it tells us how to live sexually and relationally for a divine purpose.

In the end, if we understand that "All Scripture is breathed out by God and profitable for teaching, for reproof, for correction, and for training in righteousness, that the man of God may be competent, equipped for every good work" (2 Timothy 3:16–17), then we cannot arbitrarily pick and choose what we believe is inspired. If we do, there will be little or no power for a changed heart and life. The Word of God becomes a dull butter knife, worthless in addressing the issues of the heart.

If we do not allow Scripture to define our sexuality and the sexual sin in our midst, the forces of a therapeutic culture will! The blind leading the blind. Rather, we are to make the effort to "See to it that no one takes you captive by philosophy and empty deceit, according to human tradition" (Colossians 2:8).

Freedom from Sexual Bondage

In contrast to disease theory and other human approaches, the biblical answer to sexual bondage is radical—it comes out of the promise and work of God! Everyone in sexual bondage can know this freedom: "But thanks be to God that you who were once slaves of sin have become obedient *from the heart* to the standard of teaching to which you were committed, and, having been set free from sin, have become slaves of righteousness" (Romans 6:17–18).

There are three things I want you to notice in these verses. First, freedom is for the *true* believer. This will not work if you are not born again! This is how we know if we are true believers or not: "I write these things to you *who believe in the name of the Son of God* that you may know that you have eternal life" (1 John 5:13). John is perfectly clear: "Little children, let no one deceive you. Whoever practices righteousness is righteous, as he is righteous" (1 John 3:7). Then he says, "No one born of God makes a practice of sinning, for God's seed abides in him, and he cannot keep on sinning because he has been born of God. By this it is evident who are the children of God, and who are the children of the devil: whoever does not practice righteousness is not of God, nor is the one who does not love his brother" (1 John 3:9–10).

Puritan writings were highly regarded until the nineteenth century, when they were discarded. However, since the mid-1950s and the many reprints offered by the Banner of Truth Trust, many Christians today are finding that the Puritans' deep understanding of the truth of Scripture offers guidance and understanding beyond that of contemporary writers. Thomas Watson (1620–1686) was a dedicated scholar known for soundness in doctrine. He possessed a warmth in his spirituality, and was an effective preacher and writer. His seventeen books are widely read even today. On the relationship between a Christian and sin he wrote, "Though sin lives in him, yet he does not live in sin."[9]

The apostle John in the verses cited above is making the point that you cannot be a true believer and embrace sin as a way of life. I would state it this way: you cannot be a believer, truly in Christ, and adopt sexual sin as a way of life or perpetual pattern.

We attempt to have a kinder, gentler gospel, which is not the biblical gospel. John, the apostle of love and gentleness, sees only two kinds of people: the children of God and the children of the devil. There simply isn't a third group. You are in one group or the other.

Be aware, there are false teachers today teaching that you can be righteous and yet not practice righteousness. This is a deception. No one lives a sinless life, but "Whoever practices righteousness is righteous, as he is righteous" (1 John 3:7). Redemption through the cross of Christ is a powerful reality. As Oswald Chambers put it, "Reality is not human goodness, or holiness, or heaven, or hell—it is redemption. . . . We have to get used to the revelation that redemption is the only reality."[10] Redemption goes way beyond what psychological technique can accomplish to bring about inward change, freedom from bondage, and enslavement to righteousness.

Second, we must *act* on this freedom to live as a true believer who is "obedient . . . to the standard of teaching to which you were committed"

(Romans 6:17). The opposite of slavery to sin is a commitment to real change: "For the grace of God has appeared, bringing salvation for all people, training us to renounce ungodliness and worldly passions, and to live self-controlled, upright, and godly lives in the present age" (Titus 2:11–12). *Transforming sanctification is produced by the heart-changing power of the Holy Spirit as the believer strives to live in obedience to God.*

Third, the real problem with sin, in this case sexual sin, is that it *is* sin, *and* we are guilty before a holy God. This is far more than the guilty feelings every sexual sinner experiences after the act is over. Many nonbelievers I've counseled feel tremendous guilt feelings over their sexual acts without the illumination or true conviction of the Spirit of God that brings real change. Sexual sin is a moral condition, not a psychological condition. The law has been violated, and the lawbreaker is guilty.

If we are true believers, if we act on our commitment and see our sin as true guilt before God, then there is freedom from bondage. This is *not* a freedom we create through techniques or steps. As horrible as the sin may be, the work of Christ is complete, and righteousness is imputed and imparted. God begins His work at salvation and continues His work until completion. He will not be finished until He removes both the tendency and (eventually) the possibility of sin. Complete freedom from sin comes at the resurrection of the dead. Robert Peterson makes a marvelous point: "True freedom (what I'm calling complete freedom) is the ability to love and serve God unhindered by sin."[11]

We must not waffle in our heart commitment to God's will and purpose. A man who does not clearly see his lack of commitment and still struggles with Internet pornography sent this email: "You and presumably God have some high standards. I agree that God's standard is 'not a hint [of sin],' and I agree that the core issue I have is trusting the sovereignty of God. *I say* I believe He is both sovereign and loving, but have trouble trusting my heart to some of the situations He allows in my life." Is there an *undecided* or *divided heart* in this man? He goes on to say, "I also agree that God must be a passion, *the passion* in my life. But I find myself asking 'how much is enough?' How do I balance work, church, and soccer (all things I think God wants me involved with) and still have time for God?" Some may think that I'm being too harsh on the man, but in today's spirituality we often fail to heed the warning of Jesus in the parable of the sower when He says, "The cares of the world . . . choke the word, and it proves unfruitful" (Matthew 13:22). Life has to be lived and life will often press in on us, but such "cares" can captivate the heart.

A weak commitment to God's will and purpose is subtle. The exhortation of Paul is a strong shot across the bow to those tempted to focus on worldly pursuits: "From now on, let those who have wives live as though they had none . . . those who deal with the world as though they had no dealings" (1 Corinthians 7:29, 31). We, like this man, can easily be committed to our agenda. We are tempted to privatize and individualize our Christian lives according to what we want. But selfish, privatized lives and relationships do not demonstrate the purpose of God, fail to show the glory of God, and don't point us toward the final consummation of God's plan. More often than not, our jobs, our marriages, our children, and our church all exist to serve our purpose. Christ's redemption, including sexual redemption, brings it all around to another point: "To promote good order and to secure your undivided devotion to the Lord" (1 Corinthians 7:35).

Tom and Judy arrived for our intensive counseling workshop looking like any other couple coming for help with adultery in their marriage. The difference was that Tom was still living with his girlfriend when he drove to pick up Judy to begin a week of intensive counseling. He emphatically stated up front, "When I finish this week I'm going back to the woman I'm living with."

All week long Tom listened intently and continued to indicate he was getting a lot out of the program. He did all the assignments and agreed with everything that was taught. In our last counseling session, Tom got out of his chair, fell on his knees, and in tears put his head on Judy's lap and said, "I have sinned against you, and hurt you badly, and I'm very sorry for what I've done, but tomorrow when we leave I'm going back to Cindy."

I don't know who was more in shock, Judy or me. Without question, Tom was full of knowledge—more knowledge and understanding than when he walked in the front door. In his arrogance he thanked me for all the help because it would greatly benefit his marriage to Cindy. But he wasn't truly repentant.

Such responses to the truth of God are scary. Thomas Watson puts it so well: "Learning and a bad heart is like a fair face with a cancer in the breast. Knowledge without repentance will be but a torch to light men to hell."[12]

"I Tried That; It Doesn't Work"

I've heard many wives say words like these: "John will say to me he wants to stop more than I want him to stop, but he is still looking at porn on the Internet. I don't know what I can do."

John replies, "I've tried prayer, fasting; I've pleaded with God to take this sin away. If He doesn't want me masturbating and looking at pornography, why doesn't He do something? Why did He make me this way?"

What is going on here? For one thing, I believe that God doesn't respond to selfish motives for change. If you are like John, use this question and ask God to search your heart: "Why do I want to stop looking at pornography?"

In the hundreds I've counseled struggling with pornography, hardly anyone starts getting help with right motives. Everyone gets caught and wants to stop to relieve the shame and guilty feelings, save their marriage, or keep their job. Does God answer prayers with wrong motives? No. "You ask and do not receive, because you ask wrongly, to spend it on your passions" (James 4:3).

Second, why would God take away a sin and change very little of the sinner on the inside? God is into doing a complete work of grace, not a partial one. We could have one behavior changed with the inside of the cup still remaining fairly filthy.

Third, God wants to be our God. The Lord's Prayer stresses the kingdom of God ruling and the will of God being done. God wants to change the heart, not just get rid of an uncomfortable feeling or a marriage-destroying and career-ending behavior.

Joe was a successful pastor on the West Coast, pastoring a church in a small town. He was also an exhibitionist. While in a public restroom he exposed himself to an undercover police officer and was arrested. When Joe came for counseling he was a self-centered man and God wasn't God in his life, even if he did preach every Sunday.

As God let Joe look deeper into his own heart, he clearly saw the sin of idolatry. He told me that he liked to buy expensive ties that he really couldn't afford. He would buy a new tie, bring it home, and hang it in the closet. Several weeks later, on a Sunday morning, he would put the new tie on. His wife, Carol, would ask, "Is that a new tie?" Joe would answer, "No, I've had it for a while."

Without a change of heart—where God is God, where Joe shows the fruit of being less selfish when it comes to buying ties—the sexual sin will not end because the heart has not changed. God wanted to bring real change to Joe's heart, even his motives for ministry.

So many living in sexual sin have tunnel vision. But God has the bigger picture in mind. Remember, God has given those who turn away from Him over to "the lusts of their hearts" (Romans 1:24), and He is not about to take away the loss of control if they still do "not see fit to acknowledge God"

(Romans 1:28). God must open the heart for us to see that He is not God in our lives. There must be a conviction that we have been god, not God, not only in our sexual sin but in our lives in general.

Finally, God doesn't want to take away lust without also making you a true lover, which I will cover in greater detail later.

Sam called me, having lost his marriage because his wife was fed up with the masturbation, pornography, and lack of consistent, meaningful sexual intimacy. His wife felt like sex was all about Sam, and she felt like a sexual object. He sounded desperate to change and avoid the problem in his next marriage.

When he arrived for our intensive counseling program, he told me that he almost didn't get on the plane. He said, "I read your book, *False Intimacy*, and I knew you could help me become a new man and that I would go from this place free of sexual sin. But then I realized, I didn't really want to give up 'my friend.'"

Real change is voluntary submission to the authority of God, giving Him dominion over all of life. Sam had to come to a place of knowing satisfaction in Christ and in His glory. Sam had to be willing to learn to be a lover, not a taker, in a marital relationship.

Having said all this, what if real, lasting change seems almost impossible to grasp? The Puritan John Owen (1616–1683) in his brilliant book *The Mortification of Sin* sheds more light on why people fail to see real change: "God says, 'Here is one, if he could be rid of this lust, I should never hear of him more; let him wrestle with this, or he is lost.'"[13] God's ways are not our ways. He may need to use our struggles to keep us dependent on His strength and provision.

The Sweet Fruit of Repentance

True repentance always brings the fruit of repentance, proving that the heart is now changing. That fruit is more than boasting of one's sobriety for an extended period of time. True freedom is being free from the inside to the outside.

As I travel around the country speaking to various churches and groups, the alumni of our counseling program often attend the events. When they come up to say hello, if we have some time and a private moment, I will ask them how they are doing. It may surprise you, but an adamant, "I haven't looked at porn for two years!" is not the answer I really want to hear. Yes, a man's wife desperately wants her husband to stop looking at porn, but how can she ever know he's "clean"? He has been deceiving her over and over again. There are no litmus tests for sexual purity; nor are there any completely reliable polygraph machines. While the use of torture is appealing to desperate wives, it's illegal in all marriages!

Sexual redemption is deliverance from the inside out. That filthy cup is starting to sparkle on the inside. The best answer I hear again and again as I travel and meet couples on the road is when the wife says, "My husband is a different man," or "My wife is a different woman." Yes, the behavior is gone, but the change is much deeper in the man's masculine soul and his wife can see and taste the fruit.

True repentance changes everything about the kind of person you are as a man or as a woman. This is sexual redemption and the fruit is undeniable, so there is a guarantee that God is at work. The wife is finding peace, a peace that comes from seeing the work of God manifested far beyond stopping a secret sin.

We must learn not to trust in another person, but trust in what God has done and exhibited in the fruit.

"For if you live according to the flesh you will die, but if by the Spirit you put to death the deeds of the body, you will live. For all who are led by the Spirit of God are sons of God. For you did not receive the spirit of slavery to fall back into fear, but you have received the Spirit of adoption as sons, by whom we cry, 'Abba Father'" (Romans 8:13–15). This effective redemption doesn't come through the latest self-help book or superficial techniques, but only through the creative power of redemption. The path to life is death—the death of our sin and the denial of our sinful nature.

Sexual redemption makes us different at all levels of our being. We hate sexual sin, sexual disinterest, immodesty, or anything that mars the image of God in our masculinity or femininity. We repent of all sexuality that replaces the reign of a sovereign God. And we earnestly seek to mortify all sin that was nailed to the cross when Jesus became sin for our atonement (2 Corinthians 5:21). We have to be careful here and not fall into the contemporary trap of salvation and personal relationship with Jesus as a "matter of self-improvement in order to have your best life now."[14] All of what God does is not for our satisfaction and fulfillment, but for the glory of God. With a will set free from the bondage of sin, we choose righteousness freely and enthusiastically.

Being truly repentant is daily worked out in the chaos and uncertainty of fallen circumstances and relationships. To live in a fallen world is to live in imperfect relationships, single or married, at home, at work, and at church. How do we live faithfully in all circumstances?

In the remaining chapters we will look at more of the aspects of sexual redemption lived out for the glory of God. We have been redeemed and saved from our evil ways. As Christians we don't just live our lives daily, passing through the stages of life until we enter a nursing home or the grave. We are called to live out our lives for the purpose of God. The faith that makes us completely righteous is active. We live our lives not for ourselves, but for God's purpose.

Too many Christians have goals of their own: to finish college, to have a home, to get married and have a family, to have a fulfilling career or ministry, and then sprinkle their lives with a little determination to be a Christian, hoping for the abundant life.

When I married, three days after graduating from Bible college, I had the idea of going and doing work for the Lord. I now know the truth of what Oswald Chambers said, "The work we do is of no account when compared with the compelling purpose of God. It is simply the scaffolding surrounding His work and His plan."[15]

As I have engaged with thousands of men and women from across the United States, diverse in age, in occupation, and in education, I find a common thread all the time, again stated eloquently by Chambers: "We have not yet understood all there is to know of the compelling purpose of God."[16]

I am easily moved to tears at seeing hearts and lives transformed by the power of God. It is the most amazing force! Without a doubt I have to say with Paul, "Therefore, having this ministry by the mercy of God, we do not lose heart" (2 Corinthians 4:1). In all the pain and horror of sexual sin, my heart easily leaps for joy when one sinner repents and, in newly found freedom, becomes "the righteousness of God."

The Path to Sexual Redemption

1 Have you known true repentance, or just attempted to change a behavior?

2 Why do you want to stop the insanity of sexual sin? What are your true motives?

3 If you feel you have had success in overcoming sexual sin, have others in your life noticed the fruit?

4 Have you truly offered your entire life to God, with no strings attached, so that He can transform you through your obedience?

CHAPTER TEN

Spiritual Sexuality for Men

If I venture forth alone I stumble and fall,
but on the Beloved's arms I am firm
as the eternal hills;
If left to the treachery of my heart
I shall shame thy Name,
but if enlightened, guided upheld by thy Spirit,
I shall bring thee glory.[1]

During our intensive counseling workshop, I give several lectures to the group in attendance. After my second talk, Carrie came up to speak to me. She looked less stressed than the day before.

"Dr. Schaumburg, that was really good information. I see now that maybe there is some hope for Jim and me. I didn't really understand what was going on with Jim's problem. I see that with God involved, there could be change at a deeper level. I'm praying now that Jim will find this while we're here!"

"I certainly hope you are right," I answered. "We will see how you both are doing at our next meeting tomorrow." As Jim left the classroom I thought I saw a lightness in his step.

It always amazes me how biblical truth, even though it seems tough to

121

swallow at first, brings real hope to people—even in their darkest moments. That's the life-changing power of the gospel!

In my years as a counselor dealing with sexual problems, I have been asked what feels like an infinite number of questions about sex, but invariably, at a deeper level, these questions were spiritual. Even more strangely, perhaps, when I've been asked spiritual questions, in reality they often were about sexuality! Is my experience normal or has the focus of my ministry warped my perspective?

When I started dealing with human sexuality full-time, I actually wondered if God was putting me in some sewer of humanity or at least making me deal with the seedier side of life that had almost nothing to do with Him. Now I clearly see that you can't keep God out of sex. And, to deal with sexuality is to deal with the primary spiritual issues in people's lives.

Therefore, the purpose of this book is driven by biblical conviction. I believe this book reintegrates the biblical understanding about sex into a biblical understanding about redemption. Redemption is the key to a proper understanding of sex.

Men, God, and Sexuality

Male spiritual emptiness is common. Many men, even leaders in the church, offer little in the way of spiritual nurture and protection because their own spiritual resources are depleted. Many years ago I counseled a pastor of a prominent megachurch. Every week he was teaching a seminar around the country. It seemed like everyone wanted to hear him and his principles for church growth, so he was booked two years ahead. Eventually, caught in a five-year affair, he and his wife came for our intensive counseling workshop. As his arrogance began to melt under the heat of God's light, he said to me, "Harry, every young pastor wants to talk with me and pick my brain, but if they spent fifteen minutes with me they would know that I'm spiritually empty on the inside." When you elevate your own relational desires to be loved and respected above God's desires and the needs of others, sexual temptation is nearly impossible to resist. Three times Paul says "God gave them up" (that is, those who turned away from Him) to a powerful, destructive inward desire (Romans 1:24, 26, 28) because they refused to make God the center of their lives. What then feels like a bondage to sexual sin is in fact a choice of self over God and others.

The deceitful heart does not care for others at a deep level. With no adequate theology concerning adversity in relationships, self-centeredness seems normal, even justified. So the idea of caring about your wife, especially when relational pain may result, feels completely unreasonable. The lack of caring often sounds something like this: "Why should I have to put up with this woman?"

Few men express this thought out loud, because they know they'll face the wrath of open contempt or disdain from their wife. Inside his heart and mind he feels justified in caring for himself, and false intimacy becomes a stronger temptation and may lead to bondage. Christian men don't commit sexual sin in the heart or with their body because they are wired that way; they sin sexually because they foolishly disregard God and others. Every man has one of two choices to make: The first is ignore the will of God, stubbornly follow Adam by denying your masculinity, blame your wife, justify yourself, take care of self, and become a pathetic fool.

The second choice is to follow Christ in humble submission to the will of the Father and to live to glorify the Lord Jesus with your whole body. In this way you will let "love be genuine. Abhor what is evil [on the inside too]; hold fast to what is good" (Romans 12:9). Then in the midst of any rejection, a man can choose—"To the contrary, 'if your enemy [your wife] is hungry, feed' [her]" (Romans 12:20) spiritually, sexually, and relationally. Please understand, this is not to blame the wife; selfishness was there before the wedding day and there is enough relationship struggle in the average marriage for any man to foolishly justify his actions.

If a man fails to do what is right and contrary to his selfish desires, he will "be overcome by evil" (Romans 12:21). Rather, for the glory of God, the man needs to be a spiritual, sexual, and relational blessing to his wife and others and to "overcome evil with good."

In view of Scripture, each man must courageously ask, "What do I as a man need spiritually? Where am I deficient?" Then with assertive, humble leadership he also must ask, "What does my wife need spiritually? How can I serve Christ in helping her achieve greater maturity?" Then, finally, the man should ask as a father and grandfather, "What does the next generation need spiritually?" This is the beginning of healing our male sexuality and the path to genuine manhood. Faithfulness in marriage is always about God's requirement to be a one-woman husband: No casual sexual liaisons, no flirting, no sneaking of peeks, no lustful thoughts. The bar is very high because this was the order of God from creation, and it is the only order that glorifies God.

What every man needs spiritually is a oneness with Christ—the complete oneness in which we "share his holiness" (Hebrews 12:10) and "become partakers of the divine nature" (2 Peter 1:4). If we choose this path, the image of God in us is constantly renewed in true righteousness—spiritually, sexually, and relationally. In other words, in contrast to the message of our therapeutic culture, our true need is not relational fulfillment, personal development, or satisfaction in self. Instead, what we desperately need is God-glorifying satisfaction in Christ.

Spiritual Sexuality in Our Masculinity

Spiritual sexuality begins with redemption, what I am calling sexual redemption, a "hope laid up for you in heaven" (Colossians 1:5) that flows from "the grace of God in truth" (Colossians 1:6). This grace of God brings a man to realize that his "body is not meant for sexual immorality, but for the Lord, and the Lord for the body" (1 Corinthians 6:13b). God wants his body and will collect it at the resurrection (1 Corinthians 6:14). Therefore, if your body doesn't belong to you, "glorify God in your body" (1 Corinthians 6:20). What does that look like for a man?

Undeniably, first and foremost, a man is to be sexually pure, never uniting his body with another woman other than his wife, and decisively fleeing all forms of sexual immorality (see 1 Corinthians 6:15–20). This begins before marriage and continues throughout the marriage to one woman until she dies. If a man sins, he has "an advocate with the Father, Jesus Christ the righteous. He is the propitiation for our sins" (1 John 2:1–2), including our sexual sins. From the day of illumination, true conviction, and true repentance, he will strive to live in faithfulness to God and his wife or future wife. "For this is the will of God, your sanctification: that you abstain from sexual immorality; that each one of you know how to control his own body in holiness and honor, not in the passion of lust like the Gentiles who do not know God" (1 Thessalonians 4:3–5).

There is much more to the will of God that has been revealed to us in the Word of God, and the following words, while specific to a husband, must be understood and applied to all single men as well. "For the husband is the head of the wife even as Christ is the head of the church, his body, and is himself its Savior. Now as the church submits to Christ, so also wives should submit in everything to their husbands. Husbands, love your wives, as Christ loved the church and gave himself up for her" (Ephesians 5:23–25).

How can we ignore the obvious comparisons? Like it or not, we husbands in our role are compared to Christ, while wives are compared to the church! Husbands are compared to the head; wives are compared to the body.

Then, husbands are commanded to love as Christ loved; wives are commanded to submit as the church submits to Christ. Husbands are to have leadership. Sexual redemption in Christ restores relationship between men and women in marriage in the very roles they live out. In all of the man's leadership, as we will see in a moment, he is to care for his wife and the wife is called to accept her husband's care. The family is meant to function as a spiritual unit.

Like it or not, and regardless of how badly the situation has gotten messed up, that unit has a clear authority structure.[2]

Men Are to Lead

In regard to sexuality, we all have a great responsibility to others. "See to it . . . that no one is sexually immoral" (Hebrews 12:15–16). That is a daunting task in our sexually immoral culture and church. What is required to effectively take on the challenge? I believe that the expertise required is male leadership. John Piper comments, "At the heart of mature masculinity is a sense of benevolent responsibility *to lead*, provide for and protect women in ways appropriate to a man's differing relationships."[3] This definition applies to both single and married men.

Wherever leadership is understood in marriage, application must also be made for single and married men with women other than their wives. The concept of leadership is best understood in terms of servanthood rather than dictatorial rule. Every man must acknowledge the historical abuses of the past, both in history and in our own actions, whether in our dominance or in our passivity. Many men have neglected to cherish their wives, many men have treated their wives as sexual objects, and so many of us have been too self-centered. This call for mature male leadership is not a call for dominance or an attempt to get our own way. The following nine principles formulated by John Piper further define leadership and address common misunderstandings.[4]

1. Mature leadership expresses itself not in the demand to be served, but in the strength to serve and to sacrifice for the good of the woman.
2. Mature masculinity does not assume the authority of Christ over woman, but advocates it.

3. Mature masculinity does not presume superiority, but mobilizes the strengths of others.

4. Mature masculinity does not have to initiate every action, but feels the responsibility to provide a general pattern of initiative.

5. Mature masculinity accepts the burden of the final say in disagreements between husband and wife, but does not presume to use it in every instance.

6. Mature masculinity expresses its leadership in romantic sexual relations by communicating an aura of strong and tender pursuit.

7. Mature masculinity expresses itself in a family by taking the initiative in disciplining the children when both parents are present and a family standard has been broken.

8. Mature masculinity is sensitive to cultural expressions of masculinity and adapts to them (where no sin is involved) in order to communicate to a woman that a man would like to relate not in any aggressive or perverted way, but with maturity and dignity as a man.

9. Mature masculinity recognizes that the call to leadership is a call to repentance and humility and risk-taking.

Male leadership *must* follow a biblical framework. First, with the right attitude. "Likewise, husbands, live with your wives in an understanding way, showing honor to the woman as the weaker vessel, since they are heirs with you of the grace of life, so that your prayers may not be hindered" (1 Peter 3:7). This means relating in a marriage and doing it in an understanding way. This isn't figuring women out or getting to know what makes them tick so that living together is easier. It certainty isn't passively backing down to keep the peace.

Of all the things a husband may learn about his wife over the span of marriage, this one thing stands out: understanding how God has made her beautifully vulnerable to being hurt by the husband. I've been married nearly forty years to Rosemary, and I'm a slow learner when it comes to living in an understanding way and knowing how easily I can hurt her. The reason I'm so thick headed (actually, it is a heart problem) is too often I'm thinking about how she can hurt me. It is time to be a man and demonstrate some strength and quit thinking about myself first.

Much has been said in an attempt to explain the meaning of the woman as the "weaker vessel." While the typical male is physically stronger, that doesn't fit well with the context or seem as critically important as the fact that the woman is more vulnerable to being hurt by a foolish man.

In kindness, in cherishing, and in faithfulness to his wife, a man honors her as a joint heir of grace. So many men think they seriously honor their wives by being a good provider in life and end up living out of their home as if it's a hotel with great amenities. The target is missed completely. Redefined, a good provider gives of himself spiritually to enrich and honor his wife.

In addition, a man must lead with the right style. The male style of leadership in the church gives us a good direction for style in the home. Notice the five elements of style that Paul gives Timothy. "And the Lord's servant must *not be quarrelsome* but *kind* to everyone, *able to teach*, patiently *enduring evil*, correcting his opponents with *gentleness*" (2 Timothy 2:24–25). While the passage is directed to leaders in the church, and to Timothy in particular, I believe the same leadership principles apply to marriage.

How we conduct ourselves in a quarrel, in particular what we say and how we say it, reveals much about our style of leadership. How easy it is to become huffy and sarcastic, especially if our wife's arguments don't make sense to us. I have been in so many conversations with my wife where I "knew" I was right (and many times later proven wrong) and I knew I'd regret every word I said later—but I couldn't pass up the opportunity to keep on arguing. A godly husband-leader must learn not to do that! *Don't be quarrelsome.*

The opposite of being grumpy and quarrelsome is to "be kind! Be able to teach! Be patient! Correcting gently!" Or said another way, "be Christlike." You see this demonstrated in the story of the woman at the well. Jesus was firm and direct, but there was kindness in every word, even when He was pointing out her sexual sin.

Each man must also learn to skillfully teach. Not to make his point and make his wife feel inferior, but in their life together to help bring her along as they share in the grace of God that trains us "to renounce ungodliness" (Titus 2:12). This is spiritual leadership in the home and in line with Ephesians 5 in loving a wife "as Christ loved the church."

The ESV translates the next phrase of 2 Timothy 2:24 "patiently enduring evil." What my wife says or does that seems so unfair to me is really a fight to endure, with patience, what is evil or perceived as evil at the time. The NIV reads here "not resentful." There are many sins in a marriage, but as I've seen over and over again, there is no sin that does more harm than resentment. How easily I can get offended, but how hard it is to forgive!

Finally, all leadership should be attempted *with gentleness* of spirit, which is a mildness of disposition, a meekness. The prayer from our hearts should be, "May my teaching [my instruction] drop as the rain, my speech distill as the dew, like gentle rain upon the tender grass [of my wife's heart], and like showers upon the herb" (Deuteronomy 32:2).

Leadership has tremendous power for the purpose and glory of God when a man is not resentful toward the one who has said a mean word, been disrespectful, or done something evil and malicious. Such leadership also reflects gentleness. Is this not the leadership of Christ, our great example? May God give us all more grace to live like Him.

Finally, a male leader has to have the right purpose. Ask any Christian husband, "How are you to love your wife?" and most will answer, "As Christ loved the church." It's amazing how many men get that fact right, but few men have a sound biblical idea of what that looks like. Everyone can quote that phrase from Ephesians 5 and then ignore the rest of the paragraph. Clearly, to love our wife "as Christ loved the church" means that we are to love her the *same way* as Christ loved the church. To emphasize that point, Paul repeats the concept three times in the paragraph that follows. Therefore, I conclude that everything that describes how Christ loved the church in Ephesians 5 also applies to the husband!

Love's Not Enough

Being married is more than being in love or staying in love; it has a divine purpose. A romantic date night is a great idea, but shallow when it comes to the real purpose. Sexual redemption is not primarily about a sexually and relationally fulfilling marriage. This makes more sense when you begin to understand that marriage is a metaphor of God's marriage to His people.

This is one of the most profound mysteries, as Paul calls it (Ephesians 5:32), about married life. A mystery remains hidden until the author reveals it. The plan of God was hidden until the Author fully revealed Christ. Ephesians 5:31–32 quotes Genesis 2:24, and applies the marriage relationship to Christ and the church. What is so profound is that God, in creating the one-flesh union between a man and a woman, pointed forward to Christ's union with the church, which is His "body" (Ephesians 5:23). Wow!

God is working to establish in us, His people, the standard of holiness that was found in Jesus Christ. God must work *and* we must help one another. One way He works this holiness in us is through a godly, mature marriage. The training for such a role should begin in childhood, and basic training starts in singleness lived out in godly masculinity while dating and interacting with single women.

How does a husband love his wife as Christ loved the church and be a servant-leader in marriage? First, he gives "himself up for her" (Ephesians 5:25), as Christ gave Himself up for us. The Secret Service agent assigned to the president of the United States throws himself in front of the bullet to *protect* with his life. There is no better love. "Greater love has no one than this, that someone lay down his life for his friends" (John 15:13).

If you object and say, "Not for my wife, she's not worth losing my life over," you miss the point entirely. Christ didn't lay His life down for a sweet, gorgeous woman. What would become the bride of Christ was initially a selfish, unfaithful prostitute who could have sex with you one minute and stick a knife in your back and rob you blind the next.

No husband ever has a case for not loving his wife as Christ loved the church!

Like Christ, husbands are to sacrifice their all for the purpose that you "might sanctify her" (Ephesians 5:26). Every woman, and man too, needs a major cleanup, so spiritual provision is the purpose of the sacrifice. So many men pride themselves as good providers and offer little in the way of spiritual provision. I so strongly believe in the truth of God's Word, I will insist that *a godly woman will willingly follow any man who will sacrifice everything for the purpose of his wife's spiritual well-being.* Godly women readily respond to such a man! The husband is to be in the business of helping his wife conform to the image of Christ for God's purpose and glory.

Some weak men want their wives to be all decked out and looking good, so she can be shown off in front of other men and women. That is a deep perversion of the task of helping your wife to shine for the glory of God.

Women are just as depraved as men and in need of inward heart change. They need a spiritual bath! The godly husband who is doing the right job is cleansing his wife "by the washing of water with the word" (Ephesians 5:26). This is an inward cleansing of sin, accomplished by the sound teaching of the entire inspired Word of God. "Sanctify them in the truth; your word is truth" (John 17:17). There is no excuse for physical neglect, so a man is to be a provider, but this process of loving your wife as Christ loved the church is more than the wife's temporal well-being, it is about *godliness*. It is all about the future; all about preparation for eternity.

We hear a lot about men being visual, and they are, and they should be—but with a holy focus: "so that he might present the church [the wife in the case of the husband] to himself in splendor, without spot or wrinkle or any such thing, that she [the wife in the case of the husband] might be holy and without blemish" (Ephesians 5:27). Godly male leaders look at their wives and go, "Wow! My wife is becoming brilliant in purity."

The transformation of godliness is always the work of God in our hearts and lives, single or married. To get the work done He uses vessels such as "apostles, the prophets, the evangelists, the shepherds and teachers, to equip . . . for building up the body of Christ" (Ephesians 4:11–12). There is leadership in the church for that purpose. Marriage is the creation of God for His glory, and the husband has a unique role of spiritual leadership.

Single men should start before marriage to see single women not as sexual objects to be used for pleasure but what a "splendor" they could become in the arms of a strong, godly man as they, along with a husband, uniquely display in their world the reality of the gospel. This is leadership designed with purpose in mind.

The Intimate Man

For real intimacy to occur, both spiritual leadership and unfading beauty are required. As men lead sexually, learning to be lovers and overcoming their fears of rejection, women are designed to respond. Therefore, if your wife is less interested in sexual intimacy, look no further than in the mirror.[5]

I counseled a predator who had seduced over a hundred women. He explained it was easy to do. I didn't believe him until he confessed, "I'm a con man and can convince a person of anything. If I can get a woman to talk about herself and where she's hurting, I'll convince her that I care about her. After that, sex is easy." His motives were perverted, but that man in his selfishness understood God's design for a woman, as well as God's design for male leadership and pursuit of a woman.

Understanding that about your wife, or loving your wife "in an understanding way" (1 Peter 3:7), is the real thing, and fits exactly with God's design. Try it, you'll like it!

Now if you give an honest and consistent effort to live in an understanding way and show the fruit of the Spirit in repentance for past sins—even unfaithfulness—and your wife doesn't naturally respond, there is a heart problem that needs sexual redemption. Look for a lack of forgiveness and bitterness. If your wife insists that she can't open up out of fear of being hurt, back up, but don't back away in self-pity.

Given this level of her fear, how do you continue to live in an understanding way? Go back and study Ephesians 5:25–33. Have the courage to begin to apply the framework of spiritual leadership as you care and love as Christ loved the church. Some may think me naive, but I strongly believe in the work of God in our hearts and God working through us to bring inward change outwardly expressed. This isn't the time to buy her flowers. That should come later when you celebrate the kindness of the Lord. Now is the time for confession, repentance, and moving toward your wife at the deepest level of her soul.

In many ways, the harder her heart is toward you and the truth, the easier it is to reach her heart. Dryness always produces great thirst. I believe many such women, without any awareness, have a greater vulnerability to pervert their own desires for what a godly husband has to offer and find it in the arms of another opportunistic man. If that is true, and I believe it is, there is also a great potential for God to work through a sinful husband living in obedience. Such a husband is the only man who is truly right for the job.

You Are the Man

Male leadership is never easy, but the rewards come in this life and the life to come. A wife dealing with her husband's pornography is so crushed at what he is looking at. But this is the ultimate antithesis: a man creating an image of a godly woman for God's glory and the husband seeking personal, selfish satisfaction. What woman wouldn't give anything to be a "splendor." This isn't makeup, a new figure from a new diet, or plastic surgery. It's infinitely greater.

Jeff had destroyed just about everything when he was arrested for soliciting a prostitute who turned out to be an undercover police officer. He lost his ministry and the income to provide for his family and the respect of his church, family, and friends. He almost lost his marriage to Diane. The marriage survived and Jeff supported himself working in his father's business. Men in this situation often believe they need to live the rest of their lives doing no further harm to their wives and giving them everything they want. It may sound right and the wife may enjoy all the shallow pampering, but it isn't a substitute for mature spiritual leadership. A husband-leader must always live out a holy commitment to see his wife change from the inside out to radiate the image of God.

Paul repeats the point of Ephesians 5:25 in 5:28: "In the same way" as Christ, "husbands should love their wives as their own bodies. He who loves his wife loves himself." A man may read Ephesians 5:25–27 and wonder how in the world he can be a servant-leader like Christ. Many men complain, "I never had a good role model. How can I do this?"

My standard answer to every man that says that is "You *are* a man! Christ *is* your role model. So quit whining, be a man, and get on with it." Yes, it's a hard job, but that's how men are built in the image of God. God is remaking you in His image by you accepting and living in this day-to-day challenge.

May this be our prayer:

Lord Jesus,
Grant me the favor of being led by thee,
under the directions of thy providence
and thy Word; . . .
Let thy mercy follow me while I live,
and give me aid to resign myself to thy will.[6]

The Path to Sexual Redemption

1 What do you, as a man, need spiritually? Where are you deficient?

2 What does your wife need spiritually? How can you serve Christ in helping her achieve greater maturity?

3 Can you say the above prayer from your heart? If not, why?

4 Are you ready to take the challenge of being a man and leading with humility, strength, and courage?

CHAPTER ELEVEN

Spiritual Sexuality for Women

Keep me from high thoughts of myself or my work,
for I am nothing but sin and weakness;
in me no good dwells, and my best works are but sin.
Humble me to the dust before thee.
Root and tear out the poisonous weed of self-righteousness;
keep me sensible of my sinnership.[1]

It was time to meet with Jim and Carrie again. I walked to the waiting area and saw that they were sitting in separate stuffed chairs instead of together on the made-for-two "love sofa." That told me something. If the couple is sitting together, that's often a sign that they are "getting" the gist of what I'm teaching. I did note, though, that they both looked a bit more rested than when they came for their first session—a positive sign.

We walked to my office and after the obligatory comment or two about the weather, I asked them, "Well, how's it going? What is gripping your heart this morning? Has anything happened with you relationally or spiritually?" With a smile I took a sip of my coffee and relaxed in my chair.

Carrie, looking a little agitated and sitting on the edge of her seat, jumped in first: "Dr. Schaumburg, have you read our histories?" She was referring to a form asking many detailed questions that I ask each person to fill out and return to me before our second session together. "Do you know Jim's dad was an alcoholic? Are we ignoring the importance of that?"

"Yes, I have read your histories, and I am aware of that detail from Jim's past. Why are you so concerned about that?"

"Oh, I don't know for sure. I just can't quite understand why he can't stop looking at porn." She gave Jim a glance that revealed confusion more than anger.

Typically, at this point in the process, the wife is starting to become a bit hopeful but is still filled with fear. More than likely Jim and Carrie had now had a good conversation or two, and she had heard him express something she hadn't heard before.

"Carrie, you seem a bit nervous—maybe even fearful. Am I right?" I asked.

"Well, I think we have made some progress, but how do I know if he is really changing? He has made some promises before and not kept them. How can I trust him?"

"Jim, what do you think about all this? How are you doing?" I felt it was time to get him involved.

"What you taught about this being a heart issue—that made a lot of sense to me. I think I finally am getting to the bottom of this. I have no track record. I've been a law to myself; everything has been about me. But I can understand why Carrie feels like she does."

"No, you don't!" Carrie said, crossing her legs forcefully while wrenching the cap off her water bottle.

I ignored Carrie's response for the moment to finish up with Jim. I asked Jim if he played chess and he indicated that he did.

"Have you ever played chess against the computer?" I asked.

"Yes, the computer always wins!"

"Jim, the game is over, you have already lost; playing against God, against His laws, you will always lose. It's time to surrender completely to God's will; to surrender your will."

"You know, Dr. Schaumburg, you can be a spiritual leader in the church without truly living for the will of God. I think I get the point: I don't belong to myself; now I have to live in obedience."

Looking directly into Jim's eyes, I gave him an affirming nod. Then I turned to Carrie and asked, "Carrie, what is it you really fear? And, are you giving God enough credit? He seems to be moving in Jim's life. Are you ignoring what may be happening?"

She didn't answer right away. Then her tears started to flow. I directed her attention to the box of tissue nearby. I understood how vulnerable she probably felt. What she thought had been a safe world had been ripped apart. Could she even dare to believe that a better world might come as a result of all this pain? She needed to move closer to the reassuring arms of her Father God *and* into the arms of the man who had hurt her most. But that move was hers to make.

The proper beginning point in understanding a woman's spiritual sexuality is to know her origin and position in Christ. The fatal error of our time is that we focus first on the pain of lost intimacy and then go about attempting to control our relationships. We marvel at all the beauty that God has created, but a woman remade in the image of God is even more impressive! Through the uniqueness of her femininity, she reveals something of God's glory that no one else can.

Lydia was a hardworking, dedicated wife and mother who honored her wedding vows. For thirty-five years she had believed that her husband Howard, too, was faithful to her and their covenant, but then she discovered his affair with her best friend. Howard's confession revealed a long history of unfaithfulness. She was crushed and wanted to die. Not that she wanted physical death; she just didn't want to ever again feel such emotional pain.

Lydia was no stranger to hard times and disappointment. Howard had always provided for the family but believed that the less you said, especially to your wife, the less you got in trouble. Their relationship was never truly intimate, and Lydia never felt cherished by Howard. In reality, she had lived most of her married life largely numb to that very desire. She tried counseling, but the internal conflict never left. Deep inside she wanted one thing, and she couldn't get it.

After she found out about the affair, she reasoned quite logically, "I'll make a life for myself," but her soul, with desires that never die, still led her back to her basic longing. Many well-meaning friends and others advising her said she should make a life of her own. She was also thinking about her approaching retirement. Should she retire with Howard, her enemy? How could she live with a man who had hurt her so deeply, and could do it again? But how could she live alone? Not just physically alone, but alone on the inside? How could she live with the unmet need to be cherished and not crumble beneath the agony of unmet desire?

Author Henri Nouwen looked at this question from a different perspective: "What to do with this inner wound that is so easily touched and starts to bleeding again? I don't think this wound—this immense need for affection [*to be cherished*], and this immense fear of rejection—will ever go away. It is there to stay, but maybe for a good reason. Perhaps it's a gateway to my salvation, a door to glory, and a passage to freedom."[2]

Listening to the Right Voice

At the beginning and throughout history, God has spoken (Hebrews 1:1–2) and revealed His will to all people. He is never without a voice, especially today, because God has "spoken to us by his Son" (Hebrews 1:2). Listening well, followed by obedience, was required of Adam and Eve. But their rebellion in the garden led to death. A similar scene is played out again and again in the choices we make. How do we progress from believing in and following the will of God to unfaithfulness to Christ and to one another? By listening to the wrong voice and wrong message. Like Eve, we are vulnerable to our enemy who whispers, "Did God actually say, 'You shall not eat of any tree in the garden'?" Questioning the Word of God weakens our confidence in the Word spoken and the authority behind the Word.

The desire to be rational and wise in our own understanding about life and how it works sets us up to question the wisdom of an infinite God and opens us to disobey His will.

The commands of God should not be reduced to questions, however polite and abstractly innocent they appear. *What seems reasonable to us, particularly when formulated in a question, may cause us to doubt the motives, kindness, and sincerity of God.* Once led astray at that level, when it comes to sin, we can begin to deny God's sovereign reign and the truthfulness of His will. We are then deceived into believing that the threat from God is not real, and accept the possibility that there really are not any consequences for disobedience. The heart and mind now accepts the same old lie that deceived Adam and Eve: "You will not surely die" (Genesis 3:4).

Desires are the strongest when we face difficult circumstances and are willing to do anything to escape them. Temptation becomes irresistible when the seeming reasonableness of our choice will fulfill our deepest longings and there seems to be no other course to follow.

When we are hurting, we tend to rely more on common sense than to be dependent on God. Common sense, though, doesn't factor in the selfishness of our sinful nature. A proverb points to the reality of the human heart:

"There is a way that seems right to a man, but its end is the way to death" (Proverbs 14:12). Especially when it's the shortcut out of a bad situation.

In relationally difficult times, a friend, counselor, or pastor may inadvertently play the role of the tempter. "Would God want you to suffer like this in your marriage?" the person asks. The wife listens to the question and its implications with curiosity and interest. Her internal response is, "How can I leave him, I took a vow until death?"

The tempter returns in the voice of the advisor. "Remember, you have grounds for divorce." The woman is not sure the advice she's hearing is valid, but there is a desire to be free of the pain or to find a level of comfort. Little does she see her increasing vulnerability to the kindness and the arms of a caring counselor, a deceitful predator, even a loving friend. There's also the lure of serial monogamy—start over with a new "soul mate," a lover who "truly understands me."

I'm sure for many my statements raise some questions, so at this point in the book it is a good idea to express further thoughts on divorce and remarriage. In thirty years of counseling ministry, the word *divorce* for me carries a tremendous sense of sorrow, tragedy, anger, guilt, and disappointment. I often think that death of a spouse or of a child is the only thing more devastating than divorce. Death is a hard pain and final; divorce is a pain that opens and reopens the relational wound. And from my experience and what I understand from the Word of God, it tears at the very fabric of masculinity and femininity. The process of divorce takes forever, brings dramatic change, lingering guilt, and a unique loneliness along with ongoing issues over custody, stepparents, and money. To all this reality I have seen two good responses in the church. In the majority of cases there can be the offer of loving support, guidance, and reaching out to the divorced. The other approach is rare and easily misunderstood. In this case we must teach a hatred of divorce (not the divorcee) and explain biblically why it is not God's will. Make no mistake, divorce will happen, people will insist that's it is the right thing to do, and the devastation will continue on into the next generation. Frankly, we need both responses in our day and age to do the job right for the Lord's glory.

From scriptural study I came to believe years ago the profound words of John Piper:

> The meaning of marriage is such that human beings cannot legitimately break it. *The ultimate meaning of marriage is the representation of the covenant-keeping love between Christ and his*

church. To live this truth, and to show this truth, is what it means, most deeply, to be married. This is the ultimate reason why marriage exists. There are other reasons, but this is the main one.

Therefore, if Christ ever abandons and discards his church, then a man may divorce his wife. And if the blood-bought church, under the new covenant, ever ceases to be the bride of Christ, then a wife may legitimately divorce her husband. But as long as Christ keeps his covenant with church, and as long as the church, by the omnipotent grace of God, remains the chosen people of Christ, then the very meaning of marriage will include: *What God has joined, only God can separate.*[3]

In my heart, my mind, and almost in my body, I can feel the hurt and the tragedy of the seriousness of breaking up the work of God. We all must learn to grieve the magnitude of what we have done and what others have done! And then we must cry out for mercy for ourselves and those around us.

Jesus and Paul, not surprisingly, agree on this matter. The one flesh of marriage is not our creation by planning and participating in our wedding day. *The union is the work of God the Father, not the bridegroom, nor the bride, and not even the minister.* Mark 10:8–9 states, "'And the two shall become one flesh.' So they are no longer two but one flesh. What therefore God has joined together, let not man separate." Few words could be more magnificent and startling to a Christian couple on their wedding day and throughout their marriage.

Having given some food for thought, I want to return to the main thrust of this chapter. A more comprehensive position on divorce can be found in appendix 5.

Another apparent alternative to reconciliation with her husband is for a woman to shut down her God-designed desires with a deadness that destroys the soul, and her femininity. Yet the drive to control the pain is self-defeating, because it leads to greater and greater pain. Compelled to control the situation, and the man who hurt her, she experiences a heart sickness that can only spread more and more into her being.

Lydia was one of the most angry, bitter women I've ever met. She was full of resentment and unforgiveness toward her husband. When I met the couple for counseling, Howard and Lydia had lived in unresolved anger and betrayal for twenty years following his affair with Lydia's best friend. I gently asked her, "Lydia, have you ever forgiven Howard?" Her answer startled me. With a contorted face and spitting venom, she said defiantly, "Yes, back in 1988!" which was when she first discovered the unfaithfulness.

I will go so far as to say that a forgiving woman of God should have an attitude in all relational difficulties that God will protect her so she can be what God created her to be in spite of the pain. If anyone evades pain, refusing to deal with it, there is a foolishness that blocks an understanding of "what the will of the Lord is" (Ephesians 5:17). Jesus' teaching on forgiveness overrides our contemporary therapeutic concept of looking out for ourselves in this life and instead focuses on our restored relationship with God: "For if you forgive others their trespasses, your heavenly Father will also forgive you, but if you do not forgive others their trespasses, neither will your Father forgive your trespasses" (Matthew 6:14–15).

God fulfilled His purpose through the spectacular sin of Joseph's brothers. In all occurrences of sin, including sinful betrayal, huge issues are at stake for everyone involved, including unborn grandchildren. Joseph's mean brothers wanted to kill the dream and the dreamer. But God reigns, not chance. In their vicious attempt to destroy their brother, the angry, jealous siblings helped to fulfill Joseph's dreams. Their vile act of sin against their own flesh and blood was an act created in the deceitful selfishness of their hearts. At the same time, making use of the same wicked act, God's purpose was for good: "As for you, you meant evil against me, but God meant it for good" (Genesis 50:20). This verse says "that in the very act of evil, there were two different designs: In the sinful act, *they* were designing evil, and in the same sinful act, *God* was designing good."[4]

Likewise, in the case of Howard's actions against Lydia, God had similar good plans in store for them. God reigns, not chance, and God in His infinite wisdom "meant it for good." Pain is a judgment of God, a fact of life, and just because we don't want it, there is no point in saying it should not happen. Humility realizes that God hasn't made a mistake, nor is He guilty of mismanagement. Sexual redemption is built on the foundation of sovereign grace. What does God want to teach us about Himself and godliness even in the horror of marital unfaithfulness?

Spiritual Sexuality in Femininity

The circumstance of being one with Christ is initiated by the Lord. He is the head of the church and has taken the lead. We as the church submit to Christ (Ephesians 5:24). Male leadership, doing it as Christ does it, takes the initiative for creating holy one-flesh unity within the marriage. As the church responds, so the wife responds to the husband in submission.

We are all guilty of deceitful hearts prone to listen to the things we want to hear. The eye of reason in our pain can blind us and we are left in darkness. The toughest type of couple to counsel is the pair where each spouse thinks the other person needs to listen and change. So many times in counseling I see God working right before my eyes in a man's heart and life as illumination, true conviction, and true repentance take place. Then the wife says in a brittle tone, sounding more like the man's mother, "Do *you* understand what Dr. Schaumburg is saying to *you*?" As her words spew out of her mouth, she turns away, arms folding, with a look that says, "He'll never get it!"

What disturbs me deeply is not just that she is discounting her husband but that she is brushing aside the work of God in his life. There are times in the life of a woman where God is speaking to her heart. But this is a time to stop listening for her husband to respond to her way of thinking, and instead listen to God.

Submit to *Him*?

The concept of submission can be so distasteful when we don't see and know the work of the grace of God. Ephesians 5:22–24 is the command of God, not a human author, teacher, or counselor. We cannot afford, except to our detriment, to ignore the unique role of a husband to lead and the unique response of a wife to submit. "Wives, submit to your own husbands, as to the Lord. For the husband is the head of the wife even as Christ is the head of the church, his body, and is himself its Savior. Now as the church submits to Christ, so also wives should submit in everything to their husbands" (Ephesians 5:22–24).

Just a simple reading of this passage, regardless of painful experiences from men, indicates a wife can no more avoid this response to her husband than anyone should avoid this response to Christ. Christ and the church are not in mutual submission. According to Ephesians 5:22–23, husbands have responsibilities like those of Christ, while wives have responsibilities like those of the church. The responsibilities are not simply interchangeable, any more than the roles of Christ and the church are interchangeable.

The Bible thus moves us away from any pure reciprocity in the roles of husbands and wives. The husband grows in the imitation of the love of Christ and the wife grows in imitation of the submission of the church. The roles of husband and wife are not reversible. Dr. Vern S. Poythress, professor of New Testament interpretation at Westminster Seminary, says, "The Bible contradicts the radical egalitarian philosophy that says men and women are interchangeable in virtually all respects and that their roles ought to have no relation to their sexual constitution."[5]

Mature Femininity

The response to the will of God is mature femininity. "At the heart of mature femininity," writes John Piper, "is a freeing disposition to affirm, receive and nurture strength and leadership from worthy men in ways appropriate to a woman's differing relationships."[6] Peter provides a great framework for the mature feminine response. "Likewise, wives, be subject to your own husbands" (1 Peter 3:1). The word "likewise" refers back to the general principle of submission in 2:13. A person's submission is "for the Lord's sake" because it commends Christ to others, and in this case to a disobedient husband.

In Peter's day, in ancient Roman culture, women were expected to follow the religion of their husband. If they converted to Christianity, they were like an adulteress, unfaithful to their husbands and a disgrace to the family name. In such a difficult position, what would a godly response be? The wife is primarily concerned with truth being presented to a hardened sinner. Like the wife of an unfaithful husband, who is disobedient to the Word of God, this is a daunting task. But there is a God!

A 1 Peter 3 Woman

> Likewise, wives, be subject to your own husbands, so that even if some do not obey the word, they may be won without a word by the conduct of their wives, when they see your respectful and pure conduct. Do not let your adorning be external—the braiding of hair and the putting on of gold jewelry, or the clothing you wear—but let your adorning be the hidden person of the heart with the imperishable beauty of a gentle and quiet spirit, which in God's sight is very precious. For this is how the holy women who hoped in God used to adorn themselves, by submitting to their own husbands,

as Sarah obeyed Abraham, calling him lord. And you are her children, if you do good and do not fear anything that is frightening. (1 Peter 3:1–6)

There is a time to be quiet, to not say a word, when silence speaks loudly. "They may be won without a word" (v. 1). *The loudest word ever spoken comes from a woman with respect and pure conduct whom God uses to illuminate the hard heart to pay attention to the truth.* This is feminine power at its best—power for the glory of God.

Here in 1 Peter, we see again that men are visual: they are supposed to be—and God notices true beauty too! In our sexually warped visual culture we have deteriorated to where men are looking with lustful intent and women are being immodest to create the lustful look. Two questions: Do we believe the authority of the Word of God? What really gets a man's attention? The external demonstration is to be the silence of "a gentle and quiet spirit" (v. 4).

Contrary to everything we think and many do, it is not the external appearance that makes the difference. Looking really good would actually defeat the purpose of God if it did not display "imperishable beauty" (v. 4).

I don't believe in formulas to overcome the sin in the heart, but this is extremely close to a practical application for a life committed to sexual redemption. If you are a woman whose husband has been unfaithful in either heart or physical adultery, give him what he can't resist, because in the real world of God's making and as a true believer, you have what it takes; you can "compete" from the inside out. Be that woman who displays imperishable inner beauty!

I can hear the objection of the wife who says, "But I tried that and it didn't work."

My first response is that I see women often having the wrong motive in trying to do this. You can try to be a 1 Peter 3 woman so that your husband is no longer unfaithful and you are free from further pain and the destruction of your family life. Or, you can try this approach because you hate the sin that is destroying your husband's soul. Make no assumptions about your motives: ask God to show you your heart's true condition.

Second, and likely tied to the first, how long have you been a respectful and pure woman? A 1 Peter 3 woman is a woman changing in her heart and outwardly showing the fruit of that change. This isn't something quick or done for a moment to achieve a personal goal. But it's for a lifetime for God's glory, because the "hidden person of the heart with the imperishable beauty of a gentle and quiet spirit . . . is very precious" (v. 4) to a husband. And more importantly, it is revealed "in God's sight."

So many wives say to me, "I can't change him; it's not my job to change him," and then they decide to back away to avoid more pain and disappointment. I understand the response and at one level I can agree. On another level I would in kindness disagree. The right motive *is* to change a husband, not just for personal needs, but for the higher purpose of God who is at work in a husband's heart—while at the same time *being* a woman who honors God. Therefore, there is no end point or giving up just because things look dark on the horizon. Often, the temptation to give up is driven by the thought, "This isn't working the way I want and need it to." The sin of others against us, with all its impurity and injustice, can only be clearly and compassionately seen through the eyes of a godly woman who sees herself as a sinner saved by grace. Scripture calls us to bear "with one another and, if one has a complaint against another, forgiving each other; as the Lord has forgiven you, so you also must forgive" (Colossians 3:13). Without this perspective, the offended party will find it nearly impossible to offer grace and forgiveness.

May this be your prayer:

> *Continue to teach me that Christ's righteousness*
> *satisfies justice and evidences thy love;*
> *Help me to make use of it by faith as the ground*
> *of my peace and of thy favor and acceptance,*
> *so that I may live always near the cross.*
> *It is not feeling the Spirit that proves*
> *my saved state but the truth of what*
> *Christ did perfectly for me;*
> *All holiness in him is by faith made mine,*
> *as If I have done it;*
> *Therefore I see the use of his righteousness,*
> *for satisfaction to divine justice and making me righteous.*
> *It is not inner sensation that makes Christ's death mine*
> *for that may be delusion, being without the Word,*
> *but his death apprehended by my faith,*
> *and so testified by Word and Spirit.*

The Path to Sexual Redemption

1 How vulnerable do you feel around your husband? If single, do you feel too vulnerable to a man if the relationship becomes serious?

2 Does the weakness and failures of your husband or father create a determination to control the pain?

3 Do you find the idea of a gentle and quiet spirit attractive or dangerous? Why or why not?

4 In all honestly, do you tend to respond to situations in fear or "hope in God" (1 Peter 3:5–6)?

CHAPTER TWELVE

The Seven Principles of Spiritual Sexuality

I can give myself to thee with all my heart,
to be thine for ever.
In prayer I can place all my concerns in thy hands,
to be entirely at thy disposal,
having no will or interest of my own.[1]

With Carrie dabbing her eyes and obviously not wanting to say much more until she composed herself, I turned my attention back to Jim.

"Jim, how do you respond to Carrie's fear that nothing is really changing with you?"

"Dr. Schaumburg, I know, so help me God, that I am changing! I know how much I've messed up, but it's harder to press on when your wife is uncertain. But I can understand why she feels like she does. Honey, you can trust me!" he said, reaching to touch her hand. Carrie did not respond, physically or verbally.

"I wish she would at least give me some credit!" Jim fell back in his chair, looking to me for some support. I had something else in mind.

"Jim, when you leave here in a few minutes, you have the rest of the day to move toward her instead of running. You need to be the man and hear her out. Listen to her pain and anger. Take it! Don't back away! If Carrie is willing, can you do that?"

"Yeah, I guess so," Jim answered lamely.

"You can do it, Jim. With Christ's help, you can be a leader in your marriage. This is your first opportunity to put into practice what you have learned while here, to show her you can be the kind of strong man Carrie needs. Don't wimp out and pull away! This is a time for true repentance."

"He'll only do it because you told him!" Carrie blurted.

"You need to give him a chance," I responded to her. "If he's sincere, you both will know it."

Our time was up, and as they left, I prayed that God would assist them. This might be one of the worst—and best—days of their marriage.

It's a sad turn of events, but contemporary Christians have succeeded in breaking down the barrier that distinguishes them from the world around them. Too often, our focus is not godliness but spirituality-lite. I describe spirituality-lite as happiness without peace and joy, entertainment without satisfaction, and self-centered relationships without purpose.

Contentment, as opposed to happiness, is actually a function of sanctification. The obedience of faith is made possible by grace, which allows us to resist the troubling effects of sin in our lives, and in particular sexual sin. Rather than seeking happiness on our terms, which leads to exhaustion, constant disappointment, self-pity, and further self-absorption, we must follow the instructions of our Lord and Savior: "As the Father has loved me, so have I loved you. Abide in my love. If you *keep my commandments*, you will abide in my love, just as I have kept my Father's commandments and abide in his love. These things I have spoken to you, *that my joy may be in you, and that your joy may be full*" (John 15:9–11). This is a single-minded faithful commitment that results in joy and peace.

This calling is never more faithfully expressed than when we live out mature biblical masculinity and femininity. It is imperative that a foundation of Scripture be built into our lives. If sexual redemption is taking hold, we are not to "be foolish, but understand what the will of the Lord is" (Ephesians 5:17).

Growing up in a pastor's home, I understood the will of God to be all about making the right decisions: Go to the right school; pursue the right career; marry the right person. If you don't get it right, you are out of the will of God.

As I've matured, my view of the will of God has dramatically changed. I believe that Scripture indicates that a true believer is becoming mature spiritually, sexually, and relationally, because the sovereign Lord is working inwardly in the heart. This individual is obedient to God's revealed moral will wherever he or she is geographically, relationally, or vocationally. Thus the various life choices (school, job, mate, etc.) are not as important as living a life of faith and holiness.[2]

The primary "God-help" book is the Bible. If we are to move more and more into spiritual sexuality as a man or woman, there are seven basic scriptural principles to live by. From that foundation more will come, but these principles are a critical starting point. Sexual redemption brings us into a structural framework to "walk in a manner worthy of the Lord, fully pleasing to him, bearing fruit in every good work and increasing in the knowledge of God" (Colossians 1:10). That is a very good thing! Let's look at seven principles that are the infrastructure of a vibrant spiritual sexuality.

Principle One: Eat Meat

> About this we have much to say, and it is hard to explain, since you have become dull of hearing. For though by this time you ought to be teachers, you need someone to teach you again the basic principles of the oracles of God. You need milk, not solid food, for everyone who lives on milk is unskilled in the word of righteousness, since he is a child. But solid food is for the mature, for those who have their powers of discernment trained by constant practice to distinguish good from evil. (Hebrews 5:11–14)

It's an offensive way to put it, but nevertheless true: There are too many adult Christians sucking on baby bottles. "You need milk" (v. 12b) is not a good assessment for someone who has been a believer for some time. With sin on the inside, you and I have to keep to this strict diet or the results are serious, for we are "unskilled in the word of righteousness" (v. 13). On the positive side, a consistent diet of solid food—meat—gives us "powers of discernment" (v. 14) in a therapeutic, sexually saturated culture where you need "by constant practice to distinguish good from evil."

The first principle has three goals:

- To be skilled in the word of righteousness
- To have the powers of discernment
- To distinguish good from evil

Principle Two: Train in Receiving Grace

> For the grace of God has appeared, bringing salvation for all people, training us to renounce ungodliness and worldly passions, and to live self-controlled, upright, and godly lives in the present age. (Titus 2:11–12)

Sexual redemption is a deep work of God that produces a rigorous training in the grace of God. Grace, as we have said, is not cheap; it has to cost you. By the grace of God you give up a life lived as your own god and live instead for the true God on His terms. The grace of God that shows mercy to all who were under His wrath achieves three goals:

- To renounce ungodliness
- To renounce worldly passions
- To live self-controlled, upright, and godly lives

Waiting is the key, as we'll see in more detail below. Impatient people take life into their own hands, thus becoming their own god. True believers have a living hope in an actual God.

Principle Three: Prepare Your Heart for the Long Haul

> You also, be patient. Establish your hearts, for the coming of the Lord is at hand. Do not grumble against one another, brothers, so that you may not be judged; behold, the Judge is standing at the door. As an example of suffering and patience, brothers, take the prophets who spoke in the name of the Lord. Behold, we consider those blessed who remained steadfast. You have heard of the steadfastness of Job, and you have seen the purpose of the Lord, how the Lord is compassionate and merciful. (James 5:8–11)

If evil thoughts, adultery, sexual immorality, and even murder come from inside, from the heart (Matthew 15:19), then James and Paul rightly exhort us to have a well-established heart. Paul emphasizes both the work of God and our responsibility "so that he may establish your hearts blameless in holiness before our God and Father, at the coming of our Lord Jesus with all his saints" (1 Thessalonians 3:13). God will produce the necessary sexual holiness. At the same time, Paul commands the Thessalonians to live in sexual purity. "For this is the will of God, your sanctification: that you abstain from sexual immorality" (1 Thessalonians 4:3). So we must find comfort and assurance in God's sovereignty (see Romans 8:28–30), that the sexual sin will not have control and that God will fulfill his plan for our lives.

Today, we have lost the important perspective of the return of Christ that both of these apostles emphasized. After all, it has been over two thousand years; how is that "at hand"? Peter responds by readjusting our scale of time: "with the Lord one day is as a thousand years, and a thousand years as one day" (2 Peter 3:8). We are asking, like an impatient child, "Are we there yet?" and it has only been just over two days since the Lord ascended. The small delay is for one reason: God wants as many as possible to "reach repentance" (2 Peter 3:9).

Paul connects the established heart to holiness, good works, and good words, and James sees the goals in an established heart as:

- To not grumble
- To be patient
- To remain steadfast

Without an established heart, we live in perturbed self-absorption. We live impatiently, not waiting for God's promised vindication (see James 5:1–7), and take the situation into our own hands—from aggressively using all sorts of improvement technology to better our lives, to finding escape, to practicing serial monogamy. But the correct path is building an established heart, which is a long-term, ongoing process that requires godly patience.

Principle Four: Supplement Your Faith

For this very reason, make every effort to supplement your faith with virtue, and virtue with knowledge, and knowledge with self-control, and self-control with steadfastness, and steadfastness with godliness, and godliness with brotherly affection, and brotherly affection with love. For if these qualities are yours and are increasing, they keep you from being ineffective or unfruitful in the knowledge of our Lord Jesus Christ. For whoever lacks these qualities is so nearsighted that he is blind, having forgotten that he was cleansed from his former sins. Therefore, brothers, be all the more diligent to make your calling and election sure, for if you practice these qualities you will never fall. For in this way there will be richly provided for you an entrance into the eternal kingdom of our Lord and Savior Jesus Christ. (2 Peter 1:5–11)

Redemption, which goes inwardly into our sexual being, has "granted to us all things that pertain to life and godliness" (2 Peter 1:3). With redemption there is really nothing else we need, for we have "his precious and very great promises" that will allow us to have the unthinkable: to "become partakers of the divine nature" (v. 4). If that is the case, we have to get serious about our faith and "make every effort to supplement your faith" with the particular qualities of "virtue, virtue with knowledge, and knowledge with self-control, and self-control with steadfastness, and steadfastness with godliness, and godliness with brotherly affection, and brotherly affection with love" (vv. 5–7). The goals for supplementing our faith are:

- To increase godly qualities
- To not lack godly qualities
- To practice godly qualities

Salvation is by grace alone, and entirely God's initiative. These "qualities" are not some legalistic formula for life. Rather, like the fruit of the Spirit (Galatians 5:22), they display a transformed heart. God works, and we have a responsibility to act like Jesus and follow what His Word teaches. Each true believer will express, concretely, the life of Christ as a pattern of growth and more and more exhibit "these qualities." The warning is disturbing. If we "lack these qualities" we are spiritually "blind" and have forgotten our redemption. Let us remember that in sanctification He brings us to the highest standard of holiness by putting us to work.[3]

Principle Five: Get Rid of "Other Things"

Put to death therefore what is earthly in you: sexual immorality, impurity, passion, evil desire, and covetousness, which is idolatry. On account of these the wrath of God is coming. In these you too once walked, when you were living in them. But now you must put them all away: anger, wrath, malice, slander, and obscene talk from your mouth. Do not lie to one another, seeing that you have put off the old self with its practices and have put on the new self, which is being renewed in knowledge after the image of its creator. Here there is not Greek and Jew, circumcised and uncircumcised, barbarian, Scythian, slave, free; but Christ is all, and in all. Put on then, as God's chosen ones, holy and beloved, compassionate hearts, kindness, humility, meekness, and patience, bearing with one another and, if one has a complaint against another, forgiving each other; as the Lord has forgiven you, so you also must forgive. And above all these put on love, which binds everything together in perfect harmony. (Colossians 3:5–14)

Inward change is expressed outwardly and is a strict departure from the old life. "Raised with Christ, seek[ing] the things that are above" (Colossians 3:1), we start setting our "minds on things that are above" (Colossians 3:2). Otherwise, we risk falling prey to "the cares of the world and the deceitfulness of riches" (Matthew 13:22). Perhaps this is the main reason too many find the Word of God of little value. The Scriptures lose something when such things "choke the word, and it proves unfruitful."

When sexuality is less than holy and God-honoring, look first at the influence of other things. In this principle, where we depart from the old self, the goals are:

- To put away and put off the old self
- To put on the new self
- To put to death what is earthly

Principle Six: Be Diligent

Therefore we must pay much closer attention to what we have heard, lest we drift away from it. . . . Take care, brothers, lest there be in any of you an evil, unbelieving heart, leading you to fall away from the living God. (Hebrews 2:1; 3:12)

It is easy to slack off and neglect our salvation given the "deceitfulness of sin" (Hebrews 3:13). Rest is later; work is now. "Let us therefore strive to enter that rest, so that no one may fall by the same sort of disobedience" (Hebrews 4:11) of faithlessness that occurred in the wilderness generation.

This principle has the goals:

- To avoid unbelief
- To not be hardened
- To be firm to the end

Principle Seven: Live for Others

> See to it that no one fails to obtain the grace of God; that
> no "root of bitterness" springs up and causes trouble, and
> by it many become defiled; that no one is sexually immoral
> or unholy like Esau, who sold his birthright for a single meal.
> (Hebrews 12:15–16)

None of us can make the journey alone. Individual spirituality and god-liness must not isolate us from fellowship where we have serious responsibility for others. In fact, the first six principles are practiced for the sake of others and the glory of God, not just for personal improvement.

All true believers are to be messengers who demonstrate the reality of the power of God to free them from the bondage of sin, including sexual sin. We must help one another rebuild the wall between the world's patterns and practices of sexuality and those of God's kingdom. Godly masculinity and femininity prove there can be freedom from the slavery of sexual sin and self-absorption. Godliness must be more than a personal blessing, but a message of hope with a grace that does not create the burden of impossible rules. Specifically the goals of this principle are:

- To see to it that no one fails to obtain the grace of God
- To see to it that no root of bitterness springs up and causes trouble
- To see to it that no one is sexually immoral
- To see to it that no one is unholy like Esau

That final goal pulls together all seven of the principles in a serious warning. We know the story of how Esau traded his birthright for a bowl of food. We don't want to be so foolish and do the same thing. When Tom, a pastor, is dissatisfied with his wife sexually and relationally and goes on-line to find a woman and have an affair, he is ignoring his inheritance and the blessings of the Lord—fully intending to get what he wants with another woman. When he is caught, he "repents" like Esau, with tears, which often means he wants to get back what he lost (a position of respect, income, fulfilling ministry), but is not truly sorry for his sins. We too have "an inheritance that is imperishable, undefiled, and unfading" (1 Peter 1:4), so we must not take it lightly.

As true believers we are to delight in the knowledge and love of God. We find fulfillment, joy, and peace as we "walk in love. As Christ loved us and gave himself up for us" (Ephesians 5:2).

You will find what you are truly looking for in your sexuality and life when you "walk in a manner worthy of the calling to which you have been called, with all humility and gentleness, with patience, bearing with one another in love, eager to maintain the unity of the Spirit in the bond of peace" (Ephesians 4:1–3).

We will do this knowing that we live in a world of sexual sin, and our commitment to God and others will involve suffering and sacrifice. But in so doing we will enter the joy of our Master, as we align our lives with the purposes of God.

The Path to Sexual Redemption

1 Which of the seven principles of spiritual sexuality have you neglected? In what areas do you still need growth?

2 God's ultimate purpose for you is not sexual redemption, but to live "to the praise of his glory" (Ephesians 1:12–13). Are you ready to make that commitment?

3 We don't sit back and do nothing on the soft cushion of grace. Instead, we are to "walk in a manner worthy of the calling to which you have been called" (Ephesians 4:1). For the next seven weeks focus on one principle a week and pray for God to work in your heart.

CHAPTER THIRTEEN

Married and Intimate

When faith sleeps, my heart becomes
an unclean thing,
the fount of every loathsome desire,
the cage of unclean lust
all fluttering to escape,
the noxious tree of deadly fruit,
the open wayside of earthy tares.
Lord, awake faith to put forth its strength
until all heaven fills my soul
and all impurity is cast out[1]

It was time for my next appointment with Jim and Carrie. Yesterday I had seen them from a distance on what seemed like a long walk. I'd noted that Jim had his arm around Carrie's shoulder, and from a distance it appeared that she had turned toward him and smiled.

When I entered the waiting room, the two were seated on the love sofa, holding hands. We said hello, commented on the weather, and situated ourselves in my office. Both were sitting more erect, and I sensed some new energy in their body language.

I started with my standard "brilliant" therapist question: "Well, how's it going?"

"I'll start," Jim said, reaching to touch Carrie's arm. "After reading some more and hearing your talks, I am even more convinced that my problem is much different than I thought."

"How's that?"

"This is not just my behavior out of control, but I've got to get myself squared away spiritually and right with God. I've been doing a lot of praying. I think there really is hope for me—and us!" He looked at Carrie and smiled, and reached again to touch her arm.

I turned to Carrie: "As you are listening to him, Carrie, talk about being encouraged and having some hope, what's going through your mind?"

"I go back and forth, honestly. I really want to believe this is happening, but I'm still scared." It was her turn to reach and touch Jim's arm. "But I really like what is happening so far."

"What is it you like?" I asked.

"He is listening to me. The other day after we saw you, we went back to our room. Jim asked me to 'get it all out.' So I did! I screamed at him and cried for about two hours. And he didn't get angry or leave! He just listened. And then there was the best part . . ." Carrie choked up and the tears started flowing. Jim handed her the tissue box and once again touched her arm.

"I'm sorry," Carrie said. "I'm a crier. Well, after I finished shouting at him, he came over and held me. I didn't know if I wanted him to do that, but when he did, it felt good. We've had some good talks since then—not so much screaming!" She forced a smile.

"I've been a fool," Jim said, "and I didn't want to take a look at myself, let alone change my attitude toward Carrie. But that's changing."

I looked at Jim and saw some signs of confidence in him. I knew God had answered my prayer. These two were "getting it" and on their way to sexual redemption.

What does intimacy look like in a sexually redeemed marriage?

The underlying selfishness of all premarital sex, affairs, and all forms of sexual immorality, but in particular pornography, will surface in the act of sexual intimacy within marriage. Sex may be innate to the human body and mind, but lovemaking in marriage is not instinctive to fallen men or women. It is a learning and growing process over many years within the private exclusive walls of marital intimacy.

Lovemaking is never a technique nor manipulative. Neither should there be the idolization of sex or relationship in marriage. Therefore, there is much to unlearn, and more to learn in the lifetime of each married couple. Sexual redemption renews the intimacy men and women were created to enjoy in marriage. Sexual intimacy is not a false intimacy but real intimacy. The importance of battling sexual temptation is matched by the essential struggle to learn to be lovers for life.

I do have some words of caution and concern.[2] I know that for some men and women, reading this will be very challenging. Years of hurt, guilt, and shame have taken their toll because of what you have done sexually or what has been done to you. Scripture can be misused by sinful, unloving men who make sexual demands or lewd comments, misusing their own bodies and misusing the bodies of others. There is nothing in biblical, God-glorifying sex that says take whatever you want and use it for your own pleasure.

This book, and this chapter in particular, are not armchair therapy or theology, but built on the authority of the Word of God and countless hours trudging through the trenches of sinful sexuality, sexual dissatisfaction, sexual dysfunction, and weak expressions of masculinity and femininity. The battle in the heart is the work of God. With His purpose in mind, the battle in marriage for holy sexual intimacy is the battle we are called to fight, *and* an experience we are expected to enjoy.

Marriage and the Glory of God

Meaningful sexual intimacy and relational fulfillment are not the moral standard of a godly marriage. A "good marriage" may be an excuse to withdraw into your own couple world, where you are not interested in others and focus solely on each other to get personal fulfillment. It may sound like you are giving to each other, but in reality it is the *taking* that is meaningful.

Happiness in marriage has become the custom-built plan for many couples. Couples will do anything and spend anything to maintain the fantasy. But the plan hasn't made most couples happier. In their illusion of happiness, below the surface there is little that is motivated by the principle of "for better or worse." This approach often leads to serial monogamy (sequential marital relationships motivated by selfish goals). Boredom, demanding careers, a sick child, the death of a child, financial crisis, and other challenges easily crush this type of marriage.

I've learned in thousands of hours of marriage counseling that most people believe relationship is the primary purpose. In such marriages, one or the other spouse, if not both, have developed unrealistic expectations. We may have progressed from a time when economic needs kept an essentially meaningless marriage together. I fear, though, that we have now come to expect too much happiness in this life. Some marriages are a leech-on-leech relationship. The ends of a leech look the same, with no other function than to take. Great is the expectation; great is the dissatisfaction

Sin always replaces the Creator with self. The selfishness in the heart living in the difficulties of a fallen world, without sexual redemption, will always put self first. We see our needs first, others' needs, if at all, second. Sexual redemption places proper order and value in the One loved (God), not on self, and then on the loved one (spouse).

"Sex and marriage first" always ends up asking the wrong question: "How can I feel more in love?" "How can we communicate better?" "How do we handle conflicts?" "How can we have better sex?" Sexual redemption allows us to ask the right question: "How can we serve God better through our marriage and in our sexual intimacy?" Out of meaningful sexual intimacy—and fulfilling relationship for a purpose other than self—we serve God better.

I think there is a profound connection between meaningful work outside the home, meaningful relationship, and meaningful sex within the marriage. If God is not the purpose for all three, one or the other is less fulfilling and less God-glorifying. God designed it all: Satisfaction in God, regardless of the circumstances, leads to satisfaction in others. Satisfaction in self leads to perpetual *dissatisfaction*. Then in the end, eternal distruction.

The choice comes down to this: Sex for self or sex for the glory of God. Relationship for self or relationship for the glory of God. We are called to "work the garden" of our wife's heart and mind, and to "work the garden" of our husband's heart and mind so that we may lay at our Lord's feet the fruits that have grown in His garden.

Real Intimacy

The sex scenes in R-rated movies are not the place to learn about lovemaking. Making love in marriage should be a spiritual activity, not the indulgence of self-pleasure.

Starting in childhood, Belinda had been sexually abused by her father with inappropriate touching that progressed to sexual intercourse in her teens. In high school she was promiscuous and at sixteen she was pregnant with her first child. At twenty she became pregnant with her second child on a first date. Still promiscuous in her mid-twenties, she met Troy and became pregnant with her third child. Troy admitted in counseling that their relationship was only physical, but he insisted on marrying Belinda.

In their late twenties they came for Biblical Intensive Counseling. In the first counseling session, they told me that they fought constantly, had no meaningful relationship, and actually hated each other. Their description of their marriage was tragic—one of the worst marriages I've ever seen. After thirty minutes of describing their nightmare, however, they told me sex wasn't a problem. In fact, they said they had a great sex life!

Most couples who are that conflicted and emotionally distant have no sexual relationship. Of course, "great sex" is a relative term and ranges from illicit sex outside of marriage to the meaningful sexual intimacy of a couple in their seventies. For Belinda and Troy, sex was often a twice-daily event, extremely pleasurable, and totally physical. All accomplished in a horrible relationship.

In reality, their sexual relationship was destructive, a false intimacy where each one was admittedly using the other's body for themselves. Their relationship was nothing more than vaginal masturbation. Belinda was pleasuring herself; Troy pleasuring himself. In so doing, they increase their sexual excitement and become more and more dependent on living in a fantasy.

I knew I was making headway when Troy came to their next counseling session alone and reported that Belinda had refused to get out of bed and was extremely angry. Sex was no longer happening like before. She came to the subsequent counseling session and expressed her anger to me: "You have taken away the only thing I had in life."

I explained that, in fact, that was my objective so she could find repentance and see the change that sexual redemption would bring with a new relationship with real intimacy. As God worked in her heart, she responded, wanting to know God, to let God be God, and have that kind of intimacy with Troy.

A man and a woman in an affair, even if they call it love and are experiencing some level of relationship, are still using each other because they have turned away from God and their spouse and have selfishly taken what they should have found within the marriage. Dating and engaged couples having sex do the same thing, no matter how deeply in love.

You can only find meaningful love and real intimacy in a marriage *with a divine purpose built on sexual redemption.*

Today, feeding our selfishness, we have often put sex first, which leads to "justified" sexual immorality. In marriage men have often put sex first, which has led to the wife feeling like a sexual object. An overreaction is to turn around and put relationship first, assuming that it is better than putting sex first. This creates another monster: legalized selfishness in the form of serial monogamy. Then we wonder why marriages fail and people think divorce is reasonable when they aren't happy. With relational fulfillment as the primary goal, adultery makes sense to the deceitful heart in a relationally empty marriage. If I can't find what I want with my wife/husband, I can find it with another woman/man either in fantasy, emotionally, and/or physically.

Experience and my understanding of biblical sexuality also suggest that only in God-honoring marital sexual intimacy, built on the foundation of sexual redemption, can couples avoid serious sexual problems and/or disaster. If a couple uses each other before marriage, whether in an affair that leads to marriage or premarital sex, it is a steep uphill battle to establish real intimacy, and certainly not possible without sexual redemption.

The good news is—whatever your sexual experience—there is hope! God is at work to change us inwardly from the heart, deep within our sexual being, to the outward expression of sexuality for His glory. But first we must establish the right purpose for sex and relationship.

The Right Purpose for Sexual Intimacy

In Bible college I told the Lord that He could use me any way He wanted. I didn't have a girlfriend or even a prospect of one, but I knew that I needed a wife to not be alone and find sexual and relational fulfillment. More importantly, it was essential to find someone to share in work for the glory of God. I wanted intimacy. I wanted friendship. I wanted one woman. *And*, I wanted a suitable helper.

Rosemary and I met on campus at the beginning of my junior year. The connection relationally was immediately beyond any relationship I had ever known. I knew I was in love with Rosemary as the relationship grew, but we spent hours talking about serving the Lord, the seriousness of our calling, and the importance of sacrifice without limits. In our discussions of the future, we were unconsciously moving toward marriage with a purpose.

It sounds outrageous now as I think about it that I would tell the woman I loved and wanted to marry that there would be no diamond ring to wear because where we were headed in the future, such opulence would be out of place. Over the years in my love for my wife, I often regretted that decision, but my reasons seemed valid at the time.

As we planned our wedding, we believed that our marriage was not for ourselves or for our sexual or relational fulfillment. We wanted everyone to know that our marriage was for a purpose, so our wedding invitation said: "Mrs. Philip Lundman requests the honour of your presence at the marriage of her daughter Rosemary Ellen to Reverend Harry William Schaumburg when they are united as one with Christ for service."

We were serious about sex and relationship as service and marriage with a purpose, so it wasn't difficult three years later to sell all our wedding gifts, and everything we owned, and buy a one-way ticket to Kabul, Afghanistan, with a grand total of seventy-five dollars a month in pledged support. That was 1972, when Muslim fanatics in the country were murdering infidels as a righteous act.

As I look back over forty years of marriage, I now understand that sex and relationship with a purpose beyond ourselves is the foundation that got us through all the challenges and difficulties that destroy so many marriages. Self-help books were not the answer.

The biblical purpose of marriage is a high calling. The purpose of marriage is *work for* the glory of God. It is important to review Genesis chapter 2 and notice several verses. "When no bush of the field was yet in the land and no small plant of the field had yet sprung up," there was good reason, "For the Lord God had not caused it to rain on the land, *and there was no man to work the ground*" (Genesis 2:5). Everyone knows, including God, that you don't plant a garden without water and a gardener to maintain it. "The Lord God took the man and put him in the garden of Eden *to work it and keep it*" (Genesis 2:15). Adam, now in the garden, had work to do rather than kicking back and enjoying sensual paradise.

With this in mind we can properly understand Genesis 2:18. Along with work to do as a gardener, Adam got another task—naming all the animals. Before this job was assigned, God saw that Adam needed a helper, indicating Adam's *inadequacy to do the work alone.* "It is not good that the man should be alone; I will make him a helper fit for him" (Genesis 2:18).

Many have deduced from this passage that marriage primarily solves the problem of relational loneliness. Think about it, though. Was loneliness a problem for Adam? After all, we must not forget that Adam had a special relationship with God. Scripturally, the problem of loneliness is to be met several ways. First, through relationship with God, then with friendships, including the fellowship of believers. And for most of us, through family and marriage.

Real Sexual Intimacy in Marriage

If pornography and all forms of sexual immorality pervert our understanding of sexual intimacy, we need sexual redemption for a new understanding and radical change.

I've lost count of the number of times I have been asked by couples dealing with the pangs of unfaithfulness if they should stop having sex for a while. It is an important question not to be taken lightly. This is a time where sex can be misused with great harm. Neither spouse should initiate sexual intimacy if the other is uncomfortable. The wife might buy a new sexy nighty just to hold her husband's attention. The husband may insist that he is highly sexual and pressure his wife so he doesn't have to masturbate or go outside the marriage. In the end, all of this is just false intimacy in marriage.

That said, please understand that God-glorifying real intimacy is *the* God-ordained path to healing and purity. God's gift of sex is designed for comfort, intimacy, pleasure, procreation, and control of sexual temptation.

It is tragic and shallow if an engaged couple coming into their wedding night just see sexual intimacy as now permissible. Something is lost if passionate lovemaking is not seen and realized as a part of God's created order. More tragic is a spouse who feels sex must now be tolerated rather than knowing that God is encouraging the couple to enjoy lovemaking completely.

A man and a woman looking for a spouse had a huge pool of potential mates but ended up choosing each other. In reality, *God put them together.* Being in bed for love creates a new exclusive bond for life. That bond is all the more rich when you know that God is present and seeing the goodness of your erotic satisfaction. This union is to continue until death separates the couple or age and health become an issue.

God-glorifying lovemaking is to be expected and celebrated. It is exciting, pleasurable, intoxicating, powerful, and unifying at the deepest spiritual level. Sexual intimacy may be briefly put aside for prayer, *but prayer and Bible study are not more important than holy, sexual intimacy.*

Foreplay begins *before* a kiss, a hug, a touch, or a caress. Meaningful physical foreplay and lovemaking must be preceded by touching each other's hearts and minds. There are many expressions of this type of foreplay—from pouring a cup of coffee in the morning to sharing what God's Word has spoken to your heart. True intimacy begins on the right footing. This is very true for women, but also true for men. Without this beginning the misuse of sexuality is a distinct likelihood.

In the relationship torn asunder by unfaithfulness, such "touching" is mandatory. Nothing is more powerful than understanding words with a lingering hug from a repentant man who has betrayed his wife. This is God's design and powerful work! We must join Him in humble vulnerability to the union that He created for His purpose and His delight.

So many couples living apart physically and/or emotionally have arrived for our counseling workshop with the wife not wanting to be in the same bedroom and the husband keeping a safe distance to avoid rejection and further pain from his wife. When they come to understand divine encouragement and intervention; growth in godliness; caring for one another; appreciation for the other's pain and fears; and have shared their hopes and dreams, predictably they will walk into my office with a joyful countenance and say, "Do you know what happened last night, Dr. Schaumburg?" They don't have to tell me a thing: it's written on their faces, the way they look at each other and the way they reach out spontaneously for the other's hand. God has worked for His purpose and glory and delight. It's an awesome sight!

When touched inwardly, we are built to respond physically. Kissing is to be more than a casual greeting, but passionate. Touching and caressing are varied, and will not be limited to the bedroom, and are always appropriate but should never make the other person uncomfortable. It should never just be a prelude to sexual intimacy but an expression of meaningful commitment, affection, and love that fills the mind with satisfaction and gives the reassurance that you belong to each other fully and completely.

Sexual intercourse is the ultimate physical union in this lovemaking setting, the expression of godly sensual joy to the point of giving and receiving with abandonment in the harmony of the moment as man and woman serve one another in vulnerable passion. Wow! God sure knew what He was doing when He created such ecstasy!

I'll never forget the first time I saw Rosemary at the start of my first semester, 1967. I was attracted to her the moment I saw her, before I was introduced to her. The next time we happened to meet, we enjoyed being together so much we got kicked out of the library for being too noisy. That was just the beginning!

It seems like those early moments that have turned into over forty years of relationship were always about her being the only one and no one ever being better. In later years I would come to appreciate more and more that she is the gift of God, a sovereign God who knew the "us" before we were born, before our first kiss, and before our wedding night. God had a plan to bring us together before the foundation of the world for His purpose and glory, as well as for our satisfaction.

If you know what I'm talking about, rejoice and enjoy. If you are skeptical or envious, I guarantee you that you can have God-glorifying real intimacy. This is not about goal-oriented, ideal orgasms. It is about passion with a purpose. It's not about intercourse! It is about sexual redemption with all the meaning, yearning, desire, and fulfillment that God designed. Passionate, real intimacy comes from love, comfort, and commitment. Selfish, impersonal sex doesn't result in love, comfort, and commitment. When you learn to touch each other's heart and mind, regardless of the past, through God's redemptive act, you will rejoice too!

Sexual Intimacy in Marriage Is Expressed

Rich, a man in his mid-fifties, said, "I always thought having sex with my wife would fulfill me, but it never did. My wife really never wanted to be intimate. The last fifteen years of marriage—nothing. We probably had sex ten times in twenty-one years of marriage. Only when she wanted to 'make me happy,' but no intimacy. I really just would rather masturbate—I know how to stimulate myself; it is so much easier. I can masturbate for hours, and call in sick, and not go to work."

What do marriages like this and many others with unique sexual struggles need to experience?

If you are damaged in your sexuality, far from the experience of real intimacy, forgiveness will be the place to begin a new type of sexual expression. Webster defined forgiveness as "the pardon of the offender, by which he is considered and treated as not guilty."[3] Forgiveness is always painful, but especially in marriages badly scarred by unfaithfulness. Forgiveness means, instead of returning the pain, you face it with the realization that God could not forgive you without going through horrendous pain and violence. Forgiveness is restoration.

As I've discussed before, the body, a fully sexual body, is for the Lord. The Lord's body is given for our body, which as a believer is now fully redeemed and eventually will be resurrected. Now look at 1 Corinthians 7:4: "For the wife does not have authority over her own body, but the husband does. Likewise the husband does not have authority over his own body, but the wife does."

If the body is for the Lord, if the body is a member of Christ, if we are one spirit with Him, if the body is a temple of the Holy Spirit, if the body is bought at a great price, if the body is not yours, and if you are to glorify God in your body, then you have no authority over *your* own body. *Your wife does have authority. Your husband does have authority—sexually—but only in Christ.*

Under Christ's authority and work of redemption, rather than having authority over our own body, we are to meet the real intimacy and sexual needs of our spouse. "The husband should give to his wife her conjugal rights, and likewise the wife to her husband" (1 Corinthians 7:3).

Then notice these challenging words: "Do not deprive one another, except perhaps by agreement for a limited time, that you may devote yourselves to prayer; but then come together again" (1 Corinthians 7:5). If we love God and want to love one another, it starts in the marriage bed. These commandments bring us to a particular mind-set and a radical sexual other-centeredness. This involves genuine interest in each other in a spirit of giving, as a servant-lover. The attitude of the heart is, "What can I do to arouse you more, both before, during, and after lovemaking?" And a gentle willingness to never do what the other doesn't want.

Then we can understand "Do not deprive one another" (v. 5) and properly apply the rare exceptions. Denying sex and intimacy is a mutual agreement, not a unilateral decision.

The conversation might go like this: "Sue, I'd like to not have sex for a week or two."

"John, I'm sorry," Sue gently replies. "I just can't do that right now."

Then there is no depriving. If Sue does agree to no sex, it's to be the exception, not the rule. *And* only for a limited time. *And* there is to be a divine, higher purpose.

Real intimacy for the glory of God has a built-in secondary vital purpose of protection from sexual temptation. This doesn't work if you're only having sex for the sake of sex, which always leads to the lust for more and possibly for illicit sex. It will never work as prevention if the wife feels like a sexual object and lacks interest. It will powerfully work *if* a couple is "on the same page" sexually, spiritually, and relationally, enjoying the interpersonal harmony of God-given passion. If you are not there yet, may I suggest you start the delightful journey and enjoy getting there.

This is holy sexuality, this is pure sexuality, and this is an expression of sexual redemption. Sex in marriage cannot be withheld—it is a mutual duty, it is a mutual consent, and all of that only makes sense if sex is mutually satisfying.

This true, intimate love is as strong as death! "Set me as a seal upon your heart, as a seal upon your arm, for love is strong as death, jealousy is fierce as the grave. Its flashes are flashes of fire, the very flame of the Lord" (Song of Solomon 8:6). A seal was a signet, worn around the neck and hung over the heart or on an armband. In a contract, or in this case a covenant of faithfulness, the seal would be rolled over the clay on which the contract was etched. Borrowing the picture of a sealed covenant, the person is to be placed on the heart as a seal.

Intimacy in marriage is a love bound by promises, pure and unwavering. This is much more than a marriage license that allows the consummation of the marriage in a sexual act. That's like reducing real intimacy to just jumping into the sack. Rather, this love in a holy, God-honoring marriage is as strong as the powerful (but negative) experience of death.

The logical parallel with such strong love is jealousy. This is a positive fervor, pointing to the jealousy of God. For in God's love for His people, like the love in marriage, there are to be no rivals. Know this love in a moment of ecstasy, and there together, filled with satisfaction, your hearts are warmed with joy.

We shouldn't be surprised that such desire for wild love and passion can only be tamed in marriage. May the promise of God, and the promises to each other, bring us to love this well, even in the midst of all the struggles.

The Path to Sexual Redemption

1 Have you put sex and relationship first? Are you asking the wrong questions: "How can I feel more in love?" "How can we communicate better?" "How do we handle conflicts?" "How can we have better sex?" Are you ready to ask the right questions?

2 How can you serve God better through your marriage and in your sexual intimacy?

3 Husband: How committed is your wife to tame her wild love and passion in your marriage for the glory of God?

4 Wife: How committed is your husband to tame his wild love and passion in your marriage for the glory of God?

CHAPTER FOURTEEN

Joy in God—
No Matter What Comes

There is one thing that deserves my greatest care,

that calls forth my ardent desire,

That is, that I may answer the great end for which I am made—

to glorify thee who hast given me being,

and to do all the good I can for my fellow men;

Verily, life is not worth living

if it be not improved for this noble purpose.

Yet, Lord, how little is this the thought of mankind!

Most men seem to live for themselves,

without much or any regard for thy glory,

or for the good of others;

They earnestly desire and eagerly pursue

the riches, honours, pleasures of life,

as if they supposed that wealth, greatness, merriment,

could make mortal souls happy;

But, alas, what false delusive dreams are these![1]

Eighteen years with Biblical Intensive Counseling has proven that God does work in hearts, lives, and marriages in dramatic fashion, often in a short amount of time. So when I met with Jim and Carrie for the last time, the session was typical of so many.

The contentment on their faces was confirmed as they described with amazement the work of God in their hearts.

Jim started. "I understand now that there is a penalty for arrogantly ignoring God's law. It was God's choice to redeem and deliver me from this bondage I've been in for so long. I have a new understanding of His grace and I know God is changing more than my behavior."

Carrie smiled. "This has been so amazing! Not only do I see a change in Jim, but I see more of the darkness in my own heart. I've got so much to learn about God and being a godly wife. I just didn't see the hardness of my own heart. How could I have been so blind?"

After sharing their newfound hope, Jim and Carrie, as many couples do, went on to ask practical questions.

Jim, with concern in his voice, said, "Tomorrow we go back to the real world and it scares me. I can't go back to where I was; where we were when we came here. What do we do to continue on this path?" Carrie nodded with an eagerness to know the answer.

"Jim and Carrie, God has worked in your hearts; don't ever question that no matter how rough the road ahead. Your Father will discipline you for your good as Hebrews 12:10 says, 'that you might share in his holiness.' Always remember, 'work out your own salvation with fear and trembling, for it is God who works in you, both to will and to work for his good pleasure.'"

I went on to explain that they would be given follow-up material before they left for home and how important it was to do the work.

"Remember the warning of Jesus in the parable of the sower. People do hear the truth, 'but the cares of the world and the deceitfulness of riches choke the word, and it proves unfruitful.' My prayer for you is that you never forget how dangerous it is in this world."

We finished up our last session answering the question: "What do we tell our friends back at church, our kids, and our parents?" The answer is unique to each couple's situation. As we said good-bye there were hugs and tears of joy. I wondered if our paths would cross again in this life. Neither of us had any idea of the events that would bring us together again.

What is your vision of God's purpose for you?

The particulars are unique for each of us, but God's ultimate purpose is to depend on the sovereignty of God in *all* circumstances. Your situation is not mine, mine is not yours. For each of us, however, the will of God is to face *everything* with rejoicing, prayer, and thankfulness. "Rejoice always, pray without ceasing, give thanks in all circumstances; for this is the will of God in Christ Jesus for you" (1 Thessalonians 5:16–18).

A man or a woman may have little to be happy about in their marriage or in their singleness, but *joy* is based on the objective reality of the grace of God. *Prayer* is continual because we should live by prayer and providence, in utter dependence upon God, and the unfailing dependability of God regardless of our situation. No one who is alive to the reality of God lives invincible to pain, disappointment, confusion, or loss. At the same time, in life, they are not "crushed; . . . not driven to despair; . . . not forsaken; . . . not destroyed" (2 Corinthians 4:8–9). Problems come when we are not willing to be vulnerable[2] in difficult situations and dependent on His dependability.

The redeemed are to learn to trust in the reality of the presence of God. This presence is more real than the "presence of God" in a thirty-minute worship time. "Spirituality-lite" retreats from the real relational world around us to get away from what is happening. Jesus is not some personal retreat, nor "lover" that fills the emptiness of singleness or a bad marriage. Contrary to popular thinking, God doesn't want us to only use Him to get away, but to instill in us a spiritual sexuality—fully man, fully woman—for the glory of God until the end of our lives.

Life is never to be a retreat. The real meaning of "a Christian life" is that because we have eternal life, we can face anything in this life without vacillating. We do not have to be "a double-minded man, unstable in all his ways" (James 1:8). If we live our lives focusing on the reality of God and the things that are above, are fully aware that we live in a fallen state, and truly believe in our own depravity, then the problems we face will not surprise us or cause us to drift away.

I believe the things that happen in life, which are all for God's purpose, will either make us more holy or unholy, depending on whether we truly know God in His redemptive work. The resurrected life we now possess (see Colossians 3:1–4) should bring us into oneness with God's divine purpose. Keep in mind, though, that because we are sinful, God's ways often seem wrong.

At the start of my adult life, I had it wrong. I thought sacrifice in God's service was what it was all about. I now know "it" is all about fulfilling God's purpose by knowing His *revealed will* for us. If we can remain faithful to God and others in the middle of all the tragedies of life, the real goal of God's purpose is being achieved. For the child of God, whatever happens, there is a divine design for your life.

What God Do You Know?

We all make certain assumptions about an author, particularly if he is addressing the problems and struggles in our lives. I find that many assume I have never really gone through adversity. I suppose we would all like to think that someone made it through life on a smooth road avoiding all the major bumps. I'm convinced there is no such road. Thankfully, we do not go through life alone. There is a God.

I didn't always have that view. In Bible college I told God, "You can do with me whatever You want." My commitment was to be willing to serve God anywhere, doing anything. I read about missionaries like Jim Elliot and John and Betty Stam, who lost their young lives in the service of God. So given my prayer, I thought I'd die young too.[3]

God heard the prayer, but had something else in mind.

When I proposed to Rosemary, I was dead serious about my commitment to serve and do anything. I wanted her to know what she was getting herself into if she married me. "I told God He can do whatever He wants with me. The worst that could happen is that I will die young. Therefore, if you want to get married, I see two possibilities. Either you will die with me, or you will be left a widow. Do you want to get married?"

Rosemary said yes to this unromantic proposal, and three years after we married we sold everything we owned and bought a one-way ticket to Kabul, Afghanistan, to minister on the Hippie Trail. That was 1972, when a hundred thousand young Americans and Europeans were traveling overland from Istanbul to India to escape the West. Afghanistan, as it is now, was a dangerous place in those days. There were fanatical Muslims killing infidels, robbers on the roads outside of Kabul, and dysentery so severe that we each lost forty pounds in our first month in the country.

We had no financial support raised, no savings to draw on, just the daily provision of God to put food on our table to feed ourselves and the hippies living in our large rented home. We never missed a meal. Everything we did was based on the conviction that no sacrifice was too great in the service of God.

Five years later we permanently returned to the United States without a job, without money, and expecting our second child. On June 30, 1977, Rosemary give birth to a girl we named Jennifer. Born with the most severe chromosomal abnormalities, with every organ of her body deformed, our baby girl died two days later.

In this tragedy, I had only one question: *If a man is willing to do anything for God and He allows such tragedy and pain, does God even exist?* I went and sat in a park across the street from the hospital to seek an answer to my question. Five years earlier I was enrolled in a graduate program in religious studies at a liberal university, and I was accustomed to my faith being challenged every day in class—an experience that actually strengthened my faith. As I reflected on that experience, I reached the conclusion: *There is a God!*

But that led me to the next question: *What kind of God is He?* In pregnancies with this type of chromosomal abnormality the deformity of the fetus is so severe the woman's body naturally aborts the fetus within two weeks of conception. Normally, the mother never knows she was pregnant. In one out of a million cases, there is a nine-month pregnancy and some type of birth. So why were we the "lucky ones" to defy the odds? *Couldn't God have prevented a one-in-a-million tragedy? Is He good or mean?*

I decided I didn't like this kind of God, and it made no sense to serve Him ever again.

It took many years of struggling with God, or more accurately, for God to radically change my heart and come to know the providence of God in all things. What I learned is reflected in the words of Oswald Chambers: "Until we come face to face with the deepest, darkest fact of life without damaging our view of God's character, we do not yet know Him."[4]

This I know with all certainty in my mind and heart: God is good and He is all-powerful. I now know that God did not prevent the loss of our daughter, but I also know that the same God put the right doctor on duty the night we entered St. Mary's hospital in Milwaukee. I know it is God who reigns, not chance. What appear to be random events are God's divine design. That young doctor was our main source of help and encouragement in those deepest, darkest days of our lives. He was not a believer, but make no mistake, *God put him on duty!*

Most of all, this providence of God was for our good, to shape us so that we might share in His holiness (see Hebrews 12:7–11). In adversity, to the eye of reason, the providence of God feels like a night as dark as midnight. But to the eye of faith, the dawn brings light and a new day to see God's glory.

The question is for you too: What God do you know? God reveals that He is all-good and all-powerful. Even in all the tests and trials in marriage—unfaithfulness being one of the greatest—do we know the true character of God, and do we know His will for our lives?

How does God want us to live in this kind of fallen world? I believe that the Scriptures give a resounding answer, a definitive direction for every man and every woman with regard to their masculinity and femininity lived out for the glory of God. In the broad framework of marriage, a man is to love his wife in a self-sacrificial manner by giving himself up for her, following the example of Christ. A man is bound in his commitment to his wife to help her find fulfillment spiritually, sexually, and relationally in their marriage *in all circumstances*. The wife is bound in her commitment to her husband to be respectful, pure, and demonstrate the unfading beauty "of a gentle and quiet spirit" *in all circumstances*. In all adversity they are to let their "manner of life be worthy of the gospel of Christ . . . standing firm in one spirit, with one mind striving side by side for the faith of the gospel, and not frightened in anything" (Philippians 1:27–28).

> *O let my trembling soul be still,*
> *And trust Thy Wise, Thy holy will!*
> *I cannot, Lord, Thy purpose see,*
> *Yet all is well since ruled by Thee.*[5]

The Path to Sexual Redemption

1 What is your theology of adversity? Is it guided by a worldview that justifies personal comfort and a selfish commitment to your own well-being? Or, in every event, painful or pleasant, do you see the divine design?

2 Are you seeking the joy of the Lord in all circumstances?

3 Married or single, is full devotion to the Lord evident in your life, spiritually, sexually, and relationally?

CHAPTER FIFTEEN

The Next Sexual Revolution

I can give myself to thee with all my heart,
to be thine for ever.
In prayer I can place all my concerns in thy hands,
to be entirely at thy disposal,
having no will or interest of my own.
Help me to be all prayer
and never to cease praying.[1]

It had been eighteen months since I'd said good-bye to Jim and Carrie and I'd received no emails, no notes in the mail, nor phone calls on how they were doing. I often prayerfully wondered if they "got it."[2] Out of the blue, there was an urgent message to call Carrie, so I feared the worst. I finally reached her on her cell phone.

"Dr. Schaumburg, I'm devastated, our daughter Susan has had an affair! This was the same person who was so angry at Jim. I would have never imagined she would be the one to do something like this."

Carrie went on to explain that their daughter was the most committed Christian growing up of their three children. She never rebelled, was active in church, went on mission trips, witnessed to other kids at school, and they believed she was a virgin when she got married.

"I know you taught us it's not the external, but what's on the inside. But this is my baby!"

"Tell me more," I asked.

"She's a mommy blogger. She met this guy on the Internet through a comment he posted on her blog. She even told Rick, her husband, about the comment and her response. It all seemed so innocent. Turns out this man lived in the same town. She and this guy met for coffee. They talked about life, God, and their children, but three months ago they became sexually intimate. I can't believe this is happening to me *again*—to someone I really care about. And what about my grandchildren? Susan isn't sure she wants to stay in the marriage. Can you help? Jim and I will pay for the intensive counseling if Rick and Susan agree to attend."

This wouldn't be the first time I've counseled members of the same family. If I was a younger man, I suspect I'd live to be around to help many grandchildren. I believe the situation is growing more critical, so everyone must get more involved and care about those around them.

I've always wondered what it was like before the flood when 'every intention of the thoughts of man's heart was only evil continually." If we aren't there yet, we are about to find out what it was like.

Having lived in Colorado for many years, I have seen numerous bright full double rainbows against the backdrop of a dark stormy sky. Given human sinfulness, each time I see such a sight I marvel at the mercy of God in His covenant with mankind. God sees the rainbow and remembers and keeps His Word: "Whenever I bring clouds over the earth and the rainbow appears in the clouds, I will remember my covenant between me and you and all living creatures of every kind. Never again will the waters become a flood to destroy all life" (Genesis 9:14–15 NIV). I like seeing spectacular rainbows in the wicked world we live in because I know God will preserve the earth until the final judgment (2 Peter 3:7, 13). This current order of God will not end prematurely. But we have work to do!

In our current situation, are Christians less sexually pure than pastors care to admit? There are a lot of things that motivated me to write this book, but this was number one!

In over eighteen years of ministering to Christians, both leaders and laypeople, deep in sexual sin, I have concluded that Christians are less pure and pastors are avoiding this sinful reality. Admittedly, to address the problem of sin is unpopular and a messy task. Dealing with sexual sin is even more unpopular and really a dirty job. I believe it is very appealing to cordon off sexuality from the rest of the Christian's life so we can go on living the way we want.

The real danger is that we are suppressing the truth (Romans 1:18). We do this in two ways. First, ignoring the problem of sexual immorality in our midst until a case surfaces. Second, ignoring the real problem by blaming the sexual sin on bad self-image, family of origin, or past trauma. Pastors now speak the language of the therapeutic rather than the language of the gospel of true conviction, true repentance, and holy living. As a result, individual responsibility begins to diminish.

I am amazed as I listen to people from across the country as they talk and express their primary concerns. Over and over again, psychological well-being has replaced biblical holiness. People want personal, relational, and therapeutic comfort. Discipline and sacrifice are out, and with it, sexual purity that glorifies God.

If we pull back from dealing with sexuality, and sinful sexuality in particular, we have chosen the latter of two paths. The first path is repentance; the alternative, I would suggest, is the path of arrogance. Arrogance, with its self-determination, is a central part of the sinful disposition in the heart. Therefore, arrogance is very much the essence of sin. Church life and preaching are not to conform the truth of God's Word *to* our lives and our desires. Rather, they should conform our hearts, our lives, our desires—our entire sexuality—to the Word of God.

We desperately need a *different* kind of sexual revolution!

With men and women so obsessed with seeing the opposite sex as an object of selfish pleasure, we need the Truth. Without it, it will be impossible to turn back the tide of cybersex. We are dealing with more than destructive pornography or the deconstruction of the traditional family or of normal sex through the gay agenda. *We are dealing with an enemy within!* This is where the battle must be fought.

Declaring a new war on pornography isn't going to work; we know that now. Cultural wars essentially deal with the symptoms. Political changes can be overturned by a new congress or president. Strengthening family is the right idea, but it can't be self-serving or just working toward a better lifestyle. In our world of appearance, the "makeover era," we need more than a face-lift—we need a radical inward transformation of the core reality in which our thoughts, words, behavior, relationships, sexuality, and most importantly, our hearts, are changed!

So What Must Change?

Obviously, everything in contrast to the Sexual Revolution of the 1960s and '70s. What is truly different about a *new* sexual revolution? *Nothing!* This is one of the most reassuring aspects of *this* type of dramatic and far-reaching change. This is an old, old plan, not a new technique. For that reason alone you can stake your life, actually give your life, for this revolution. The plan for redemption existed before the foundation of the world—"even as he chose us in him before the foundation of the world, that we should be holy and blameless before him" (Ephesians 1:4).

Changing behavior just doesn't cut it! It is external, potentially legalistic, and just plain stupid. An unbeliever can change his or her behavior with any type or form of a higher power he or she chooses. Real power is never that nebulous and has One Source. Real power is Complete. Real power is Eternal. Real power is God-initiated. "What if God, desiring to show his wrath and *to make known his power*, has endured with much patience vessels of wrath prepared for destruction, in order to make known the riches of his glory for vessels of mercy, which he has prepared beforehand for glory" (Romans 9:22–23)? God's before-time plan included the particular goal of the ultimate overthrow of horrific human evil.

We must keep to the plan! Just because sexual sin is pervasive and destructive doesn't change the Master Plan. Stick with *the* plan! What is at stake here is the sovereignty of God over all sin. His plan is the ultimate destruction of all evil. His plan removes the wrath of God to come to all who believe. His plan forgives sin. In His plan justice is vindicated by grace, and grace alone. *Only His divine plan with the real power of God can change the sinful heart forever and ever!*

Let this sexual revolution begin in your heart!

The Only Starting Point That Works

Repentance is where we begin the internal sexual revolution. Repentance fully accepts "The message . . . that God is light, and in him is no darkness at all. If we say we have fellowship with him while we walk in darkness, we lie and do not practice the truth. But if we walk in the light, as he is in the light, we have fellowship with one another, and the blood of Jesus his Son cleanses us from all sin" (1 John 1:5–7).

In the gravity of the present crisis, it is time to "walk in the light" and live spiritually, relationally, and sexually according to the biblical vision of living in truth. In this sexual revolution, we must know the truth, but a "walking in the light" revolution will also require *being* the truth. There is no other way to live free of the bondage of sin, especially the bondage of sexual sin.

Real Power Comes from Deliverance

The ultimate bondage is not from sexuality, but death! The power of death was held by Satan. Christ came to die in order to "deliver all those who through fear of death were subject to lifelong slavery" (Hebrews 2:15). The great news is that God "has delivered us from the domain of darkness and transferred us to the kingdom of his beloved Son, in whom we have redemption, the forgiveness of sins" (Colossians 1:13–14).

Therefore, let the sexual revolution continue!

When it comes to deliverance from the bondage of sin, "you also must consider yourselves dead to sin and alive to God in Christ Jesus. . . . For sin will have no dominion over you, since you are not under law but under grace" (Romans 6:11, 14). Without redemption:

- We deserve to die as the *penalty* for sin, including sexual sin
- We deserve to bear God's *wrath* against sin, including sexual sin
- We are *separated* from God by our sins, including sexual sin
- We are in *bondage* to sin, including our sexual sin

Basic to the gospel is the understanding that we are sinners and are in bondage to sin. For many, that includes sexual sin. We need someone to provide redemption, to "redeem" us out of that bondage.

With redemption:

- We can trust in Christ for the forgiveness of sin, including our sexual sin
- Christ has paid the penalty for our sin, including our sexual sin
- The death of Christ has fully satisfied God's justice required for sin, including our sexual sin
- We are no longer in bondage to sin, including sexual sin
- We are now one spirit with Christ

Therefore, let the sexual revolution begin in you!

Real Power Is Applied Power

Modern ears prefer the sound of a gentle passive voice inviting them to God, like some Big Daddy in the heavens, where they *eventually* become sexually pure. Yes, we are absolutely justified by Christ's righteousness alone, but given our responsibility, biblically, the pressure isn't off. I understand, no one likes to be pressured; I certainly don't.

Ted was like a number of single guys I've seen in counseling: bright, successful, gifted, and good looking. Quickly stating that he was a Christian, he told me that in the impersonal hooking up scene, getting a girl to have sex was easy, even Christian girls at church. It is understood as sex with no questions, no commitment. He said, "To be honest, if it wasn't for my mom pressuring me to come to you for counseling, I wouldn't be here. I really don't feel too bad about what I'm doing. But I am concerned about marrying a godly woman and having to tell her about my past. On the other hand, I don't think I can stop. Does God even know what He is doing?"

For Ted and many others, not having sex until marriage is an archaic law. The biblical vision of sexuality can seem like a list of arbitrary rules. It can also feel like God is playing a cruel game in that He demands sexual purity and then turns around and makes us highly sexual. What gives? It is the same issue whatever the sin, whatever the temptation.

Why does "sin cling so closely" (Hebrews 12:1)? Of this I'm absolutely convinced: God cares for us at the highest level. Whatever God does, whatever God ordains, whatever God puts into motion, and however God disciplines us, it is "for our good" (Hebrews 12:10).

Our childish perspective doesn't always see that truth, so we say to ourselves and others, "What is God doing?" Yet, it is all for our good, and the only "good" that matters is "that we share his holiness" (Hebrews 12:10). Therefore "strive . . . for holiness, without which no one will see the Lord" (Hebrews 12:14). C. S. Lewis wrote of holiness, "The job will not be completed in this life: but He means to get us as far as possible before death. That is why we must not be surprised if we are in for a rough time."[3] I'd suggest that the pressure is on!

There must be the application of redemption that is *progressive* our entire life. This is the work of God *and man*. In the process we become more free from sin and like Christ. The process begins at regeneration.

The Corinthians were sexual sinners, famous for having impersonal sex in their temples. For the true believers, in regeneration, we are described by Paul this way: "And such were some of you. But you were washed, you were sanctified, you were justified in the name of the Lord Jesus Christ and by the Spirit of our God" (1 Corinthians 6:11).

In this first step, the power begins by breaking the power of sin. As a result, the person is no longer dominated by or loves his sin. *The power is now present to be "dead to sin"* (Romans 6:11): "having been set free from sin, [we] have become slaves of righteousness" (Romans 6:18). Real power applied acknowledges we will never be free of sin in this life, but a true believer doesn't wallow in self-pity and give up and say to his wife, "I've struggled with pornography for twenty years and you are just going to have to live with it until I die." The true believer's sexual desires have changed—from a love of sexual sin to hating sexual sin in self and others.

Prior to conversion we were lost, slaves to sin; there was no power to change on the inside, only on the outside. At conversion the power was real. *We were made righteous!* This was the new beginning where power is applied throughout life and the process of pursuing holiness is completed at death.

In this process God is *disciplining us* (Hebrews 12:5–11). God helps us *want His* work to be done (Philippians 2:13), and equips us to do His will (Hebrews 13:20–21). Real power is applied power with an active role as we depend on God. We present ourselves to God (Romans 6:13): We are to present our bodies "as a living sacrifice, holy and acceptable to God, which is your spiritual worship" (Romans 12:1). Obedience is our active role. We are to *strive* (Hebrews 12:14); we are to *make every effort* (2 Peter 1:5); we are to *abstain* (1 Thessalonians 4:3); and we are to *purify* ourselves (1 John 3:3).[4]

Real Power Is Power Together

In the next sexual revolution, the transformation is by God's internal power with our active participation—*but we don't do it alone!* This new revolution cannot occur through privatized spirituality or individualism. We must join forces within the body of Christ.

Today, the concept of being responsible for one another is hard for many to understand. Our culture teaches us to leave people alone, to give them their space, to let them do their own thing, to let them exercise their freedom in whatever way they want to. We are taught, certainly, to take responsibility for ourselves, but rarely for others. This individualism is deeply ingrained in our culture, in who we are by nature, and it flows out of our selfish hearts.

Responsibility for one another in marriage and in the church is not about our own insecurities, our need to control others, our tendency to project our faults onto others, or our desire to bring others down so that we can make ourselves look good and build our self-image. True believers will always be working at getting the log out of our own eye rather than getting the wood chip out of someone else's eye. The right spirit is that of a servant, willing to help. "Let each of you look not only to his own interests, but also to the interests of others" (Philippians 2:4). The approach is that of a servant.

Mobility, the Internet, and cell phones create a new type of connection; an impersonal, independent connection. For the early Christians it was very different as they focused on their community with each other. The early Christians knew that they needed each other, not just for companionship, but they had a strong sense of taking responsibility for each other—and not only their material needs—but their most deeply sinful and spiritual needs as well.

When fellow Christians went astray, other Christians would intervene in order to help them return to living a life of holiness. There was a "one anothering" tradition in the church and taught in Scripture that meant when we see a fellow Christian—a spouse, a sibling, a friend, an acquaintance—messing up, either by their words or attitudes or actions, other brothers and sisters had an obligation to point out to them the sin that had ensnared them. "Brothers, if anyone is caught in any transgression, you who are spiritual should restore him in a spirit of gentleness. Keep watch on yourself, lest you too be tempted. Bear one another's burdens, and so fulfill the law of Christ" (Galatians 6:1–2). Much of Scripture is ignored today within the church. As indicated above, the process of growing in godliness is the work of God and we are active participants in His process as we "Strive for peace with everyone, and for holiness without which no one will see the Lord" (Hebrews 12:14). The purity is given to us by God; He oversees the ongoing process by His discipline (Hebrews 12:3–11) and we do two things: "Strive for peace . . . and for holiness" (Hebrews 12:14), and second, we are responsible for one another to "See to it that no one fails to obtain the grace of God" (Hebrews 12:15).

I have often wondered what it would be like to join a local church where the elders would interview someone for membership and explain that their fellowship strongly believed in responsibility for one another and regularly practiced watching out for one another so that "no one fails to obtain the grace of God." They would address three things in that effort and expect the same three things from each member: They would start with the overriding goal to "See to it that no one fails to obtain the grace of God," then also make sure "that no 'root of bitterness' springs up and causes trouble, and by it many become defiled; that no one is sexually immoral or unholy like Esau, who sold his birthright for a single meal" (Hebrews 12:15–16).

Would you join such a church?

This is where the next sexual revolution fans out!

A church that would practice this kind of responsibility for one another would go far beyond accountability and shallow support groups. Traditional accountability is woefully inadequate for two reasons. First, you are only as accountable as you want to be. That's why every list of "tough questions" in accountability always ends up with the same two questions: "Have you just lied to me?" and "Have you just lied to me about lying to me?" Second, even if one is telling the truth, the questions and the accountability process focus on performance or behavior, not the heart.

Godly support groups with sound doctrine would greatly assist in the new revolution, but self-serving groups that rarely challenge sin and fail to encourage striving for holiness will only exacerbate the problems in marriages and the Christian community.

Revolution for the Long Haul

Up against the dominance of sexual sin in our culture, with raw, in-your-face temptation, old habits that pull us backward, fear that shrinks back from more pain, bitter discouragement, and a heart that so easily seeks immediate gratification, how does anyone fight on to the end? The central focus of encouragement must be found in One Person and the work of that Person. Christ is "the founder and perfecter of our faith" (Hebrews 12:2). Don't look around, but "lay aside every weight, and sin which clings so closely . . . looking to Jesus" (Hebrews 12:1–2). He has His eyes on you; get your eyes on Him.

Several years ago I was counseling an NFL star caught in sexual sin. He was selected to play in the Pro Bowl several times and had won a Super Bowl. I like to watch NFL football, but I think of it as just a game. He explained that it is really a show and the audience is always watching. Every moment he is on the field, playing or resting on the sidelines, he is performing for the audience with every movement of his body. Given his life of sexual sin, I explained to him he should realize that everyone else does too. We all play for an Audience of One!

Revolutionaries will remember that we are to have no fear of "those who kill the body but cannot kill the soul. Rather fear him who can destroy both soul and body in hell" (Matthew 10:28). Jesus tells us what the Audience of One is capable of, right down to the last detail. A single sparrow doesn't fall without God knowing and He even keeps count of the number of hairs we have on our heads (Matthew 10:29–30). The point is simple in its profoundness. God knows and sees everything.

If we know God, He knows us! Therefore, if we know our Audience, in this revolution we have nothing to gain, nothing to lose, and nothing to prove except to hear, "Well done, good and faithful servant." As we look to Christ, seeing all that He suffered from hostile sinners (Hebrews 12:3), we will "not grow weary or fainthearted," for we see the face of Glory. We see the One who sees us.

Let the Next Sexual Revolution Begin

We don't need more counselors, more small groups, or new techniques. What we need most we already have: the Bible, God's inspired Word, and people to do the hard work of living before God for His purpose and glory. There is no magic key or formula, but the following concepts must guide us:

- Every man, woman, and child is a sexual being. *This revolution is for everyone!*
- The commandments of the Lord are a picture of God's reality in the face of the world's madness. *This revolution has the answer!*
- In this time of cultural sexual insanity, the gospel is never more relevant. *This revolution has a foundation!*
- Restricting sexual intimacy to the faithfulness of marriage is a part of living out of the fullness of the gospel. *This revolution has a divine purpose!*
- In the gospel we stand and fight on the high ground. *This revolution is assured of victory!*
- The gospel teaching on sexuality is a message of good news. *This revolution offers living hope!*
- Holiness is where sex fits; it is the model for human sexuality. *This revolution can't fail!*
- God commanded sex to be holy to reflect His holiness and faithfulness. *In this revolution God knows what He's doing!*

I'll end with one last goad. I find that the sexual sinner, filled with wrong intentions and bad ideas, is often willing to listen. Not so the self-righteous person.

C. S. Lewis, writing on "Sexual Morality" in *Mere Christianity*, makes a provocative statement: "All the worst pleasures are purely spiritual: the pleasure of putting people in the wrong. Of bossing and patronizing and spoiling sport, and back-biting; the pleasures of power, of hatred. That is why a cold, self-righteous prig who goes regularly to church may be far nearer to hell than a prostitute. But of course, it is better to be neither."[5]

Our greatest challenge is to begin with ourselves!

Will you join me in the next sexual revolution?

> *Keep me walking steadfast towards the country*
> *of everlasting delights,*
> *that paradise-land which is my true inheritance.*
> *Support me by the strength of heaven*
> *that I may never turn back,*
> *or desire false pleasures*
> *that wilt and disappear into nothing.*
> *As I pursue my heavenly journey by thy grace,*
> *Let me be known as a man with no aim*
> *but that of a burning desire for thee,*
> *and the good and salvation*
> *of my fellow men.*[6]

The Path to Sexual Redemption

1 Are you striving for holiness? If so, what needs to change spiritually, sexually, and relationally in your life?

2 In your marriage, family, small group, and local church, are you ready to take responsibility for one another? What is your first step? When will you implement it?

3 It is hard to see self-righteousness in ourselves, especially when we are the hardest workers in the church, the most faithful in marriage, quickly discern sin in others, and feel the most spiritual. Rather than being offended by the label, or quick to assume it doesn't fit, pray: "Create in me a clean heart, O God, and renew a right spirit within me" (Psalm 51:10).

4 If God has begun a deeper work in your heart, share this book with your spouse, a friend, and someone at church. As a beginning point, talk about working together to apply the Seven Principles of Spiritual Sexuality.

Masturbation: A Form of False Intimacy

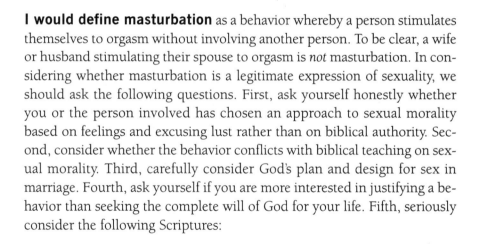

I would define masturbation as a behavior whereby a person stimulates themselves to orgasm without involving another person. To be clear, a wife or husband stimulating their spouse to orgasm is *not* masturbation. In considering whether masturbation is a legitimate expression of sexuality, we should ask the following questions. First, ask yourself honestly whether you or the person involved has chosen an approach to sexual morality based on feelings and excusing lust rather than on biblical authority. Second, consider whether the behavior conflicts with biblical teaching on sexual morality. Third, carefully consider God's plan and design for sex in marriage. Fourth, ask yourself if you are more interested in justifying a behavior than seeking the complete will of God for your life. Fifth, seriously consider the following Scriptures:

- "But put on the Lord Jesus Christ, and make no provisions for the flesh, to gratify its desires" (Romans 13:14)
- "Do not be conformed to the world" but rather "be transformed by the renewal of your mind" (Romans 12:2)
- "Put to death therefore what is earthly in you: sexual immorality, impurity, passion, evil desire, and covetousness, which is idolatry. On account of these the wrath of God is coming" (Colossians 3:5–6)
- "Abstain from the passions of the flesh" because they "wage war against your soul" (1 Peter 2:11)

- Belonging to Christ, we have "crucified the flesh with its passions and desires" (Galatians 5:24)

We are urged to "walk by the Spirit, and you will not gratify the desires of the flesh. For the desires of the flesh are against the Spirit, and the desires of the Spirit are against the flesh, for these are opposed to each other, to keep you from doing the things you want to do" (Galatians 5:16–17).

Dr. Daniel R. Heimbach[1] encourages us to consider God's plan and design for sex. He outlines God's design for sex to be "exclusive" with another person of the opposite sex, a wife or husband. God designed sex to be "profound," which masturbation is not; it is superficial. God made sex to be "fruitful," but masturbation treats sex like a thing rather than a capacity for producing human life. God made sex to be "selflessly" God-centered. Masturbation, like all false intimacy, is self-centered and self-satisfying. God made sex to be "complementary," joining husband and wife in an expression of one-flesh union: a relationship between one man and one woman for life.

Dr. Heimbach further instructs: "If masturbation refers directly to the practice by which a person brings himself or herself to orgasm without anyone else involved, then one is arousing their own male or female passions. It is non-relational, same-sex arousal. A man thinking about his wife does not make the reality of the experience heterosexual." Thus, masturbation is still outside the biblical pattern and something to be avoided in order to live consistently in the will of God and abstain from sexual immorality (1 Thessalonians 4:3).

To summarize, Dr. Heimbach's arguments clarify that masturbation is a form of false intimacy and should be considered sin. "So whoever knows the right thing to do and fails to do it, for him it is sin" (James 4:17). The following are important considerations.

- Sex is a part of a personal relationship with another person; masturbation is non-relational
- Sex is to be an exclusive, one-man, one-woman relationship; masturbation typically involves sexually impure thoughts about other people
- Sex is to be special and intimate, an expression of real intimacy; masturbation is frequent and shallow
- Sex is to be fruitful (productive) in that man is designed to enter a woman and to create, both at a relational, spiritual, and reproductive level; masturbation treats sex like a thing to be consumed

- Sex is to take place within the context of selfless love; masturbation is designed to satisfy oneself
- Sex is multi-dimensional; masturbation separates the physical from everything else
- Sex is to be complementary; masturbation is non-unitive

Ten Things to Do When Your Spouse Is Unfaithful[1]

1. Don't engage in wishful thinking; expect evil. "Do not be surprised at the fiery trial when it comes upon you to test you, as though something strange were happening to you" (1 Peter 4:12).
2. Don't turn and run; endure evil. "Love bears all things, believes all things, hopes all things, endures all things" (1 Corinthians 13:7).
3. Let your heart lead; let love be genuine and hate evil. "Let love be genuine. Abhor what is evil; hold fast to what is good" (Romans 12:9).
4. Pray and desire to be delivered from evil. "Lead us not into temptation, but deliver us from evil" (Matthew 6:13).
5. Don't seek revenge. Look for ways to feed your enemy. "'Vengeance is mine, I will repay, says the Lord.' To the contrary, 'if your enemy is hungry feed him; if he is thirsty, give him something to drink'" (Romans 12:19–20).
6. Don't hide the sexual sin, expose it. "Take no part in the unfruitful works of darkness, but instead expose them" (Ephesians 5:11).
7. Work to restore your marriage. "If anyone is caught in any transgression, you who are spiritual should restore him in a spirit of gentleness" (Galatians 6:1).

8. Respond with a purpose: Look for ways to do good. "Do not be overcome by evil, but overcome evil with good" (Romans 12:21).

9. If you are a husband, love your wife and give yourself up for her for a godly purpose. "Husbands, love your wives, as Christ loved the church and gave himself up for her; that he might sanctify her, having cleansed her by the washing of water with the word" (Ephesians 5:25–26).

10. If you are a wife, turn your disobedient husband to the Lord without a word through respectful and pure conduct. "Likewise, wives, be subject to your own husbands, so that even if some do not obey the word, they may be won without a word by the conduct of their wives—when they see your respectful and pure conduct" (1 Peter 3:1–2).

What Does It Mean to "Get It"?[1]

I strongly suspect that attempts to control sexual sin fail "to work" for most folks because they hold the assumption that changing behavior is the primary path to saving a marriage, a career, or avoiding other negative consequences that can devastate a family. However, in terms of sexual redemption, the critical questions instead are, "What does it mean for me to live for the glory of God?" and "What does it mean to 'get it'?" We shouldn't be asking, "What can we do?" but rather "Did I get it?" or, "Am I willing to do things God's way rather than my own way regardless of the pain? Am I willing to glorify God and die to self?"

So what does it mean to "get it"? Carefully read the following and let it challenge your heart. Please don't read with the idea of doing a checkup or passing a test. Rather, read with the attitude of Psalm 139:23–24 (NIV), "Search me, O God, and know my heart; test me and know my anxious thoughts. See if there is any offensive way in me and lead me in the way everlasting."

To "get it" means:

1. To break the hard outer layer of independence from God.
   Anything else is spiritual fraud.
2. To no longer follow my own ideas but choose absolute loyalty to Jesus Christ.
   This is what makes a strong believer.

3. To be broken of my own understanding of myself.
   This is nothing less than giving up my right to myself.
4. To be open to the fact of God's creative purpose—that He has created me for Himself and His glory.
   This is being open to God's purpose versus my own needs.
5. To not be overcome by anxiety, but to be absolutely confident in the Father.
   Believing that God will work all things out well.
6. A surrender of my will, not surrender to a persuasive or powerful argument.
   This is a step of faith in God and His truth.
7. Less concern for taking care of the "other things" of life.
   Seeking first the kingdom of God and His glory.
8. To not attempt to avoid relational pain, but to love God and others.
   Trusting that in losing my life, I will find it.

Some don't "get it." Why? I'm convinced that the church should be a place where people meet God and a place where God brings people He has chosen. In reality, church is an intensive care unit. This metaphor accurately describes the ministry we should do and the impact of that ministry on people's hearts and lives. Spiritually, some people live and some will die. The fellowship of believers can be a great place to be, but it is no picnic to work in an intensive care unit when you know not everyone will live, and you never know the outcome while you're doing the surgery. I keep asking myself, "Why do some people not 'get it'?" The question is an important one. Like a skilled surgeon, I am always learning. I have to constantly examine how I do my work. The Master Surgeon is watching, and I don't want anyone to perish.

After eighteen years of Biblical Intensive Counseling, this is my answer and I share it with you with the prayer that each one "gets it." I usually see one major reason people come for help with sexual sin, and two types of responses. Generally speaking, everyone who comes has in mind the pressing need to change a behavior, end an affair, and/or save a marriage. Therein lies the basic problem of getting it. We often focus on the external—the behavior and the pain—rather than the internal. What seems like a logical center of attention is filled with flawed thinking and the pervasive false teaching within the evangelical church. This leads many to spend their energy and their entire lives on "living life well." Therefore, when an affair, pornography, or some other type of sexual sin is uncovered, it threatens the goal of living an abundant, fulfilling Christian life. It prevents us from having a meaningful marriage and guarantees endless pain. The response is to do whatever must be done to recover the abundant life and get the marriage back on track. It's just common sense—but is it biblical thinking?

If we are biblically grounded, we will start from an entirely different perspective: "Our citizenship is in heaven, and from it we await a Savior, the Lord Jesus Christ" (Philippians 3:20; see Ephesians 2:19). The opposite and powerful perspective described above comes from "minds set on earthly things" (Philippians 3:19). The biblical understanding of life centers on the essential *internal* change that leads to life (Philippians 3:21) versus the *temporal* change that will fail and lead to death. Repentance is not an emotional response to sin. It is much more than behavior management or a matter of being in recovery. It is a genuine heart change that always produces a life of righteousness. God's redemptive grace requires a person's responsive obedience. Repentance is a radical inward change that results in everything else beginning to change. Repentance always bears fruit as the work of God continues and we live out our lives in a manner "worthy of the gospel of Christ" (Philippians 1:27), working out our "salvation with fear and trembling, for it is God who works in you, both to will and to work for his good pleasure" (Philippians 2:12–13). Repentance is not merely new behavior. Repentance is inward change leading to the fruit of new behavior. It is imperative that we understand that Jesus demands this inward change. In Luke 13:3 Jesus speaks with absolute clarity when He states, "No, I tell you; but unless you repent, you will all likewise perish." He then repeats the exhortation in verse 5.

So why do some people "get it" while others don't? Most come desperate to change a behavior, possibly to save a marriage, and certainly to stop the pain, but many never truly repent with an internal change of mind and heart. They leave with a false hope based on mere sorrow for their sin, a commitment to change their behavior, and a new desire to find real intimacy in their marriage. Those singles and couples die, while those who shift their perspective to the desperate need of inward change live. The former leave dependant on their good efforts; the latter leave dependant on the continued work of God. They cling to God in fear and trembling, with a desire to "walk in a manner worthy of the calling to which you have been called" (Ephesians 4:1; see Colossians 1:10; 2:6–7). God's call to internal and external righteousness is sobering; we must work hard at living the Christian life in continual obedience. That response does not merit salvation, but it does demonstrate the work of God within (Philippians 2:12–13).

Sexual Dysfunction

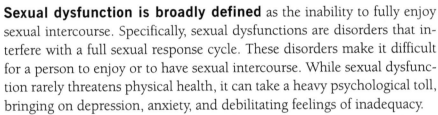

Sexual dysfunction is broadly defined as the inability to fully enjoy sexual intercourse. Specifically, sexual dysfunctions are disorders that interfere with a full sexual response cycle. These disorders make it difficult for a person to enjoy or to have sexual intercourse. While sexual dysfunction rarely threatens physical health, it can take a heavy psychological toll, bringing on depression, anxiety, and debilitating feelings of inadequacy.

Sexual dysfunction takes different forms in men and women. A dysfunction can be lifelong and always present, acquired, situational, or generalized, occurring despite the situation. A man may have a sexual problem if he:

- Ejaculates before he or his partner desires
- Does not ejaculate, or experiences delayed ejaculation
- Is unable to have an erection sufficient for pleasurable intercourse
- Feels pain during intercourse
- Lacks or loses sexual desire

A woman may have a sexual problem if she:

- Lacks or loses sexual desire
- Has difficulty achieving orgasm
- Feels anxiety during intercourse
- Feels pain during intercourse

- Feels vaginal or other muscles contract involuntarily before or during sex
- Has inadequate lubrication

The most common sexual dysfunctions in men include:

- **Erectile dysfunction:** an impairment of the erectile reflex. The man is unable to have or maintain an erection that is firm enough for coitus or intercourse
- **Premature ejaculation:** rapid ejaculation with minimal sexual stimulation before, on, or shortly after penetration and before the person wishes it
- **Ejaculatory incompetence:** the inability to ejaculate within the vagina despite a firm erection and relatively high levels of sexual arousal
- **Retarded ejaculation:** a condition in which the bladder neck does not close off properly during orgasm so that the semen spurts backward into the bladder

Until recently, it was presumed that women were less sexual than men. In the past two decades, traditional views of female sexuality were all but demolished, and women's sexual needs became accepted as legitimate in their own right.

Common female sexual dysfunctions include:

- **Sexual arousal disorder:** the inhibition of the general arousal aspect of sexual response. A woman with this disorder does not lubricate, her vagina does not swell, and the muscle that surrounds the outer third of the vagina does not tighten—a series of changes that normally prepare the body for orgasm ("the orgasmic platform"). Also, in this disorder, the woman typically does not feel erotic sensations
- **Orgasmic disorder:** the impairment of the orgasmic component of the female sexual response. The woman may be sexually aroused but never reach orgasm. Orgasmic capacity is less than would be reasonable for her age, sexual experience, and the adequacy of sexual stimulation she receives
- **Vaginismus:** a condition in which the muscles around the outer third of the vagina have involuntary spasms in response to attempts at vaginal penetration
- **Painful intercourse:** a condition that can occur at any age. Pain can

appear at the start of intercourse, midway through coital activities, at the time of orgasm, or after intercourse is completed. The pain can be felt as burning, sharp searing, or cramping; it can be external, within the vagina, or deep in the pelvic region or abdomen

A Different View on Divorce

As you read the following, keep in mind that the real purpose of marriage is to display the covenant-keeping love of God toward His people. Also, that we must not search the Scriptures to back up our theories or demands. I encourage you to read with an open heart.

So many people I have counseled in considering divorce refer to Matthew 19:9 as grounds for divorce. Starting in verse 3 we see that the Pharisees came and asked Jesus about divorce to test Him. Essentially their purpose was to get Jesus to incriminate Himself by misinterpreting the law and going against Moses. Their question was, "Is it lawful to divorce one's wife for any cause?" Like the Pharisees, we can assume we know the answer. Yet, we must see God's design and His purpose in marriage and search out and listen to God's answer. Here is the clear answer: "Have you not read that he who created them from the beginning made them male and female, and said, 'Therefore a man shall leave his father and his mother and hold fast to his wife and they shall become one flesh'" (Matthew 19:4–5). Jesus quotes Moses to them and then states His divinely authoritative interpretation of the passage. "So they are no longer two but one flesh. What therefore God has joined together, let not man separate" (v. 6). No marriage is merely the mutual agreement of a man and a woman. It is a deep and mystical union like no other human relationship that should display our union with Christ.

Simply put, Jesus' answer to the Pharisees' question is a resounding

"No!" Hearing that answer brought them to the main point of their testing of Jesus. "Why then did Moses command one to give a certificate of divorce and to send her away?" Great question, and the Lord doesn't hesitate to give a direct answer: "Because of your hardness of heart Moses allowed you to divorce your wives, but from the beginning it was not so. And I say to you: whoever divorces his wife, except for sexual immorality, and marries another, commits adultery" (Matthew 19:8–9). John Piper comments on this statement of Jesus: "This is amazing. It implies, in other words, that there are laws in the Old Testament that are not expressions of God's will for all time, but expressions of how best to manage sin in a particular people at a particular time. Divorce is never commanded and never instituted in the Old Testament. But it is permitted and regulated—like polygamy was permitted and regulated, and like certain kinds of slavery were permitted and regulated."[1] So the point that Jesus is making and that should grip our hearts is that permission to divorce is not God's ideal nor His original order. It is permitted, but points to a serious problem that is at the core of all sin: hardness of the human heart.

Here is the important question for us today given the reality of hardness of heart: Is divorce consistent with the will of God in the lives of Christians in the church age? Christ has come, and God has now spoken "to us by his Son" (Hebrews 1:2) in what are the "last days." How we live now must flow out of this big reality because "if anyone is in Christ, he is a new creation. The old has passed away, behold the new has come" (2 Corinthians 5:17).

Remember Jesus' commentary on Genesis 2:24 in Matthew 19:6: "So they are no longer two but one flesh. What therefore God has joined together, let not man separate." In this passage, the word "man" indicates all humans, not an individual male. So the point is this: More than the institution of marriage, God has created the union between a man and a woman. This mysterious union displays the greater mystery of Christ and the believer. Therefore, we do not have the right to break up what God has created for His divine purpose. What we have here is the call of our Lord to a higher standard, just as there is no right to a polygamous relationship or to enslave another human being in this age. Jesus' teachings never lowered the standard, but raised them higher and called for a radical obedience. Anger is murder; lust is adultery; and you can't require justice, as in the Old Testament (Matthew 5:21–38).

In Mark, Jesus and the disciples have a private moment in the house and they ask for clarification on the question of divorce. Jesus answers:

"Whoever divorces his wife and marries another commits adultery against her, and if she divorces her husband and marries another, she commits adultery" (Mark 10:11–12). The answer is clear and calls for a new and radical obedience.

But the question remains, Is adultery grounds for divorce based on Matthew 19:9? "And I say to you: Whoever divorces his wife, except for sexual immorality, and marries another, commits adultery." First, notice the parallel between this verse and Mark 10:11. I read this verse to say that there are grounds for *remarriage* in the case of adultery. Divorce, because of hard hearts, will be the choice of many, so the grounds for remarriage would be important. It has always amazed me how quickly we find grounds for divorce and never seek an answer to the grounds for remarriage other than our needs and happiness.

Not many today would understand Jesus' exception clause to apply primarily to remarriage. John Piper, sounding like a single voice crying in the wilderness, also argues for this interpretation. He looks at the Greek and concludes that the exception to remarriage applies to a situation like Joseph and Mary's, to those betrothed to be married, and when there is adultery in that relationship, remarriage is permitted. Piper goes on to say, "This view is not widely held. I commend it for your serious consideration."[2] I would make the same recommendation, not only on that particular verse, but on the whole question of divorce. God's standard of faithfulness can only be understood in light of His absolute, unwavering faithfulness to His betrothed (the church, the body of believers). In other words, while we await our final union with Christ, He will never "divorce" us, even when we are unfaithful—as we often are. We are to be moving toward this higher standard both spiritually in our relationship with Jesus and in our marital relationship with our spouse.

Read Matthew 19:3–14; Mark 10:2–12; Luke 16:18; Romans 7:1–16; 1 Corinthians 7:11–13. Then read John Piper's books *This Momentary Marriage* and *What Jesus Demands from the World*.

A Call to Modesty

Paul, writing to young Timothy, makes it clear that the gospel must lead to practical changes in the lives of true believers. Redemption leads to godliness in our sexuality and our relationships. For men, the besetting sin mentioned is "anger or quarreling" (1 Timothy 2:8), which is contrary to godliness. I know from personal experience that men don't like to see that in themselves. Then in verse 9 he shifts to women by saying, "likewise also." While the male issue is anger, modesty is the female issue here. Like men, women aren't always comfortable looking at their key issue. "Women should adorn themselves in respectable apparel, *with modesty and self-control*, not with braided hair and gold or pearls or costly attire, but with what is proper for women who profess godliness—with good works" (1 Timothy 2:9–10). Carolyn Mahaney, a woman speaking to women, says it better than I can:

> In his word, God commands us to pursue the beauty of modesty and self-control both in our heart and in our dress. If we earnestly apply his word in our hearts, it will be displayed by what we wear. When it comes to selecting clothes to buy and wear, however, we can often feel lost and confused. Which items are seductive and immodest and which display a heart of modesty and self-control?[1]

If we are to address the problems of men lusting and women being immodest, we must understand that while the issues are different on an external level, the core heart problem is the same for both genders. In other words, if men are inclined to look with lustful intent, woman are inclined to want a man to look. A change of heart is required for both. Both are to reveal a changed heart where men see real beauty and women show real beauty.

John MacArthur comments on this passage in 1 Timothy:

> How does a woman discern the sometimes fine line between proper dress and dressing to be the center of attention? The answer starts in the intent of the heart. A woman should examine her motives and goals for the way she dresses. Is her intent to show the grace and beauty of womanhood? . . . Is it to reveal a humble heart devoted to worshipping God? Or is it to call attention to herself, and flaunt her . . . beauty? Or worse, to attempt to allure men sexually? A woman who focuses on worshipping God will consider carefully how she is dressed, because her heart will dictate her wardrobe and appearance.[2]

Carolyn Mahaney goes on to challenge women at a heart level with these penetrating questions:[3]

- What statement does my clothes make about my heart?
- In choosing what clothes to wear today, whose attention do I desire and whose approval do I crave? Am I seeking to please God or impress others?
- Is what I wear consistent with biblical values of modesty, self-control, and respectable apparel, or does my dress reveal an inordinate identification and fascination with sinful cultural values?
- Who am I trying to identify with through my dress? Is my standard the Word of God or is it the latest fashion?
- Have I asked other godly individuals to evaluate my wardrobe?
- Does my clothing reveal an allegiance to the gospel, or is there a contradiction between my profession of faith and my practice of godliness?[4]

Recommended Resources to Walk the Path of Sexual Redemption

Books

Bennett, Arthur, ed. *The Valley of Vision: A Collection of Puritan Prayers & Devotions.* Carlisle, PA: Banner of Truth Trust, 1975.

Chambers, Oswald. *My Utmost for His Highest.* Grand Rapids, MI: Discovery House, 1992.

Elliot, Elisabeth. *Let Me Be a Woman.* Wheaton, IL: Tyndale House, 1976.

Fitzpatrick, Elyse. *Idols of the Heart: Learning to Long for God Alone.* Phillipsburg, NJ: P&R Publishing, 2001.

Heimbach, Daniel. *True Sexual Morality: Recovering Biblical Standards for a Culture in Crisis.* Wheaton, IL: Crossway Books, 2004.

Mahaney, C. J. *Sex, Romance, and the Glory of God: What Every Christian Husband Needs to Know.* Wheaton, IL: Crossway Books, 2004.

_____, ed. *Worldliness: Resisting the Seductiveness of a Fallen World.* Wheaton, IL: Crossway Books, 2008.

Peace, Martha. *Attitudes of a Transformed Heart.* Bemidji, MN: Focus Publishing, 2002.

_____. *Damsels in Distress: Biblical Solutions for Problems Women Face.* Phillipsburg, NJ: P&R Publishing, 2006.

_____. *Tying the Knot Tighter: Because Marriage Lasts a Lifetime.* Phillipsburg, NJ: P&R Publishing, 2007.

_____. *The Excellent Wife: A Biblical Perspective.* Bemidji, MN: Focus Publishing, 1995.

Piper, John. *Finally Alive: What Happens When We Are Born Again.* Geanies House, Scotland: Christian Focus Publications, 2009.

_____. *Future Grace.* Sisters, OR: Multnomah Publishing, 1995.

_____. *This Momentary Marriage: A Parable of Permanence.* Wheaton, IL: Crossway Books, 2008.

_____. *What Jesus Demands from the World.* Wheaton, IL: Crossway Books, 2006.

Piper, John and Wayne Grudem, eds. *Recovering Biblical Manhood & Womanhood: A Response to Evangelical Feminism.* Wheaton, IL: Crossway Books, 1991.

Schaumburg, Harry. *False Intimacy: Understanding the Struggle of Sexual Addiction.* Colorado Springs, CO: NavPress, 1991.

Scott, Stuart. *The Exemplary Husband: A Biblical Perspective.* Bemidji, MN: Focus Publishing, 2002.

Watson, Thomas. *The Doctrine of Repentance.* Carlisle, PA: Banner of Truth Trust, 1987.

_____. *The Godly Man's Picture.* Carlisle, PA: Banner of Truth Trust, 1992.

Welch, Edward. *Addictions: A Banquet in the Grave.* Phillipsburg, NJ: P&R Publishing, 2001.

Internet

www.desiringGod.org
www.truthforlife.org
www.settingcaptivesfree.com
www.restoringsexualpurity.org
www.challies.com
www.discerningreader.com

From the Ministry of Stone Gate Resources and Dr. Harry W. Schaumburg

1. Biblical Intensive Counseling Workshops

There are many programs and methods of help, but the uniqueness of Biblical Intensive Counseling (BIC) stands out. It is distinctly different from traditional counseling. In traditional counseling, a counselor meets with a client weekly for one hour. BIC is a full five days. The depth, complexity, ugliness, and danger of sexual sin are addressed at the level of the heart. We focus on God working to change the heart, allowing significant progress to be made in the process of sexual redemption.

With nearly three thousand alumni and eighteen years of experience, this program has proven effective in hundreds of lives and marriages. Real change means moving beyond relapses to a life free of lust, sexual addiction, pornography, and all forms of unfaithfulness. Real change through sexual redemption is *life* changing, not just a change in behavior.

www.stonegateresources.org
Toll-Free: 1-888-575-3030
Email: info@stonegateoffice.com

2. Seminars by Dr. Harry W. Schaumburg

Visit www.stonegateresources.org and click on Speaking Engagements for seminars in your area or to request a seminar be held.

3. For Individuals, Couples, and Small Groups

Sexual Redemption: Life-Changing Spirituality and Sexuality by Dr. Harry W. Schaumburg. This is a fifteen-week program utilizing *Undefiled* and numerous other resources to encourage a change of heart that transforms a person spiritually and sexually. It is designed for use by individuals, couples, and small groups. It is available online at www.restoringsexualpurity.org.

4. A Blog by Dr. Harry W. Schaumburg

www.pureheartpuremind.com

Notes

Chapter 1: Sexual Redemption?

1. Arthur Bennett, ed., *The Valley of Vision: A Collection of Puritan Prayers & Devotions* (Carlisle, PA: Banner of Truth Trust, 1975), 126.

2. Dissatisfaction does not refer to a specific sexual dysfunction, but includes disappointment with initiation patterns, arguments over frequency, and interfering aspects of anger and dissatisfaction with the after-play/afterglow experience. My experience indicates that over 80 percent of couples seeking counseling are dissatisfied sexually.

3. See appendix 4 for description.

4. Many people today have no issue with masturbation if it doesn't involve lust. Many counselors and youth pastors counsel men to masturbate rather than engage in lust. In our attempt to deal with one problem, we may be guilty of creating another. Almost every wife I've counseled is hurt by their husband masturbating and thus avoiding intimacy. Encouraging masturbation to avoid lust is questionable when there remains in the heart issues of self-centeredness and self-comfort. For further discussion, see chapter 3 and appendix 1.

5. John Piper, "Sex and the Supremacy of Christ, Part 1," *Desiring God Conference*, 24 September 2004, http://www.desiringgod.org/resourcelibrary/ConferenceMessages/ByConference/2/1657_Sex_and_the_Supremacy_of_Christ_Part_1/ (accessed May 24, 2008).

6. Biblical Intensive Counseling goes beyond recovery to offer real change, pointing people away from sexual sin to restored intimacy with God and others. The counseling is brief and intensive, allowing for significant work to be completed in a short time, and a higher level of concentration on personal issues. It is also a private, personal time to grow in the Lord, begin a process of restoration, and find hope in a setting of peace and quiet. This program has proven to be a time for healing and restoration for those who struggle with sexual sin or relational brokenness. For more information, visit www.stonegateresources.org.

Chapter 2: Revealing the Darkness

1. Arthur Bennett, ed., *The Valley of Vision: A Collection of Puritan Prayers & Devotions*, 132.

2. This is a major controversy within the church. We have lost the clear biblical understanding of the difference between men's and women's roles. As a result, many oppose any unique male leadership role in the family and in the church. This has led to men and women being unsure what their roles should be. Selfishness, irresponsibility, passivity, and in some cases abuse have distorted our thinking as it relates to the roles of men and women.

3. The way you dress is a reflection of who you are on the inside. Your dress and grooming send messages about you to others and influence the way you and others act.

4. Sex in advertising is nothing new. Advertisers have continually pushed the bounds of what they can and can't get away with, riding the line between advertising and pornography. The images of women in advertising are beautiful, sexy, and made to be appealing. It is not porn in the legal sense, but often has the same emphasis on external beauty as nudity, without the objection of being inappropriate. The ultimate issue is that what women are to be is dictated by false beauty: an external focus, which leads to discomfort with a less-than-"perfect" body. Men and women, and especially boys and girls, all need help understanding that true beauty is internal—reflected in one's character and heart. The church and Christian women must learn to seek out true beauty and demonstrate it.

5. The entire report on the worldwide pornography industry can be found at: www.toptenreviews.com/pornography. Jerry Ropelato, CEO of TopTenReviews, states, "These statistics are the most accurate and complete report of the worldwide pornography industry to date."

6. Ibid.

7. According to the information found at www.toptenreviews.com/pornography, the top five video producers are the U.S., Brazil, the Netherlands, Spain, and Japan, by companies like Playboy, Wicked Pictures, Your Choice, and Soft on Demand.

8. Ibid.

9. Ibid.

10. Ibid.

11. Ibid.

12. Ibid.

13. Sinead Carew, "Porn to Spice Up Cell," http://www.reuters.com/article/technology-News/idUSN3030000720080130?sp=true (accessed November 14, 2008).

14. Stephen Brown, "Executive Summary: Peer-to-Peer Study Results by Palisade Systems," http://palisadesys.com/news/releases/view.php?pressreleaseid=33 (accessed November 12, 2008).

15. Stephen Bagg, "Craigslist's Dirty Little Secret," April 5, 2007, http://blog.compete.com/2007/04/05/craigslist-popular-categories/ (accessed August 15, 2008).

16. Daniel Heimbach, *True Sexual Morality: Recovering Biblical Standards for a Culture in Crisis* (Wheaton, IL: Crossway Books, 2004), 345–48.

Chapter 3: The Struggle for Christians

1. Arthur Bennett, ed., *The Valley of Vision: A Collection of Puritan Prayers & Devotions,* 124.

2. Charles R. Swindoll, "An Open Letter Concerning the #1 Secret Problem in Your Church," reproduced at http://www.blazinggrace.org/cms/bg/swindoll (accessed August 1, 2008).

3. Timothy C. Morgan, "Porn's Stranglehold," *Christianity Today,* http://www.christianitytoday.com/ct/2008/march/20.7.html (accessed July 16, 2008).

4. For further thoughts on this point, see John Piper's book *Future Grace* (Sisters, OR: Multnomah, 1995), 329–38.

5. For further thoughts on masturbation see appendix 1.

6. Chris Abraham, "The Psychology of Hooking Up," http://chrisabraham.com/2006/06/01/the-psychology-of-hooking-up (accessed May 11, 2008).

7. Mark Regnerus, *Forbidden Fruit: Sex & Religion in the Lives of American Teenagers* (New York: Oxford University Press, 2007), 147–50.

8. Donna Freitas, *Sex & the Soul: Juggling Sexuality, Spirituality, Romance, and Religion on America's College Campuses* (New York: Oxford University Press, 2008), 215, 216. Freitas defines "spiritual colleges" as Catholic, nonreligious private, and public colleges and universities where the idea of the spiritual lacks structure but maintains a relationship with the divine and may cultivate a sense of higher purpose or meaning in life.

9. Regnerus, *Forbidden Fruit,* 124.

Chapter 4: Is This a Disease?

1. Arthur Bennett, ed., *The Valley of Vision: A Collection of Puritan Prayers & Devotions,* 127.

2. Daniel G. Amen, "Sex on the Brain: Seven Tips to Enhance Your Love Life," *Christian Counseling Today* 15, no. 4 (2007): 16.

3. Os Guinness, personal conversation, May 2, 2006.

4. Os Guinness and John Sell, eds., *No God but God* (Chicago: Moody, 1992), 95.

5. Ibid., 106.

6. Edward Welch, *Addictions: A Banquet in the Grave* (Phillipsburg, NJ: P&R, 2001), 28.

7. Mark Laaser, *The Secret Sin: Healing the Wounds of Sexual Addiction* (Grand Rapids, MI: Zondervan, 1992), 22.

Chapter 5: Why Is Sex Such a Big Deal?

1. Arthur Bennett, ed., *The Valley of Vision: A Collection of Puritan Prayers & Devotions,* 143.

2. Most biblical scholars see human marriage as temporary, yet it points to something that will be a permanent reality: the relationship between Christ and the church. With eternal life, the need to procreate will end, and we can assume that marriage and sex will no longer be necessary in our immortal state.

3. John Piper, "I Will Not Be Enslaved by Anything," http://www.desiringgod.org/ResourceLibrary/Sermons/ByDate/1985/505_I_Will_Not_Be_Enslaved_by_Anything/ (accessed June 4, 2008).

4. John Piper, *This Momentary Marriage: A Parable of Permanence* (Wheaton, IL: Crossway Books, 2009), 14.

5. Ibid., 15.

6. Ibid., 131.

Chapter 6: The Missing Male

1. Arthur Bennett, ed., *The Valley of Vision: A Collection of Puritan Prayers & Devotions*, 223.

2. John Piper, *This Momentary Marriage: A Parable of Permanence* (Wheaton, IL: Crossway Books, 2009), 26.

3. Joseph Weber, Amy Barrett, Michael Mandel, and Jeff Laderman, "The New Era of Lifestyle Drugs," *BusinessWeek*, http://www.businessweek.com/1998/19/topstory.htm (accessed November 16, 2008).

4. "Erectile Dysfunction/Impotence," Methodist Hospital System, http://www.methodisthealth.com/tmhs/basic.do?channelId=-1073830978&contentId=1073790771&contentType=HEALTHTOPIC_CONTENT_TYPE (accessed November 16, 2008).

5. God's command to Adam assumes his ability to choose and his moral responsibility. The command was given to Adam prior to Eve's creation, implying a leadership role for "the man" that also included responsibility to "keep" (Genesis 2:15) all of creation.

6. Both "man" and "you" are singular in Hebrew.

7. John E. Hartley, *The New International Commentary: Genesis* (Peabody, MA: Hendrickson Publishers, 2000), 67, 68.

8. "The woman and the man are not cursed (it is unthinking to speak of their malediction!); but severe afflictions and terrible contradiction now break upon" them. Gerhard Von Rad, *Genesis: A Commentary* (Philadelphia: Westminster Press, 1972), 93.

Chapter 7: The Hardened Female

1. Arthur Bennett, ed., *The Valley of Vision: A Collection of Puritan Prayers & Devotions*, 181.

2. For a detailed exploration of mature masculinity and femininity, to which I owe much of my thought and conviction, see John Piper and Wayne Grudem, *Recovering Biblical Manhood & Womanhood* (Wheaton, IL: Crossway Books, 1991), 31–59.

3. Ibid., 229.

4. Serial monogamy is defined as being faithful to your current partner or spouse as long as the relationship fulfills your purpose. If it doesn't, the individual moves on to the next partner or spouse. For example, I once counseled a woman in her fifth marriage. While she had never committed adultery, I asked her, "Are you going to be faithful in *this* marriage?"

5. Oswald Chambers, *My Utmost for His Highest* (Grand Rapids, MI: Discovery House, 1992), October 5.

Chapter 8: The Real Problem

1. Arthur Bennett, ed., *The Valley of Vision: A Collection of Puritan Prayers & Devotions*, 218.

2. Sinclair B. Ferguson, *The Sermon on the Mount* (Carlisle, PA: Banner of Truth Trust, 1987), 87.

3. Ibid., 86.

4. John Piper, *What Jesus Demands from the World* (Wheaton, IL: Crossway Books, 2006), 209.

5. Ibid.

6. Ibid., 210.

7. John Piper, *Future Grace* (Sisters, OR: Multnomah Publishers, 1995), 331.

8. John Calvin, *Commentaries on the Epistles of Paul to the Galatians and Ephesians* (Grand Rapids, MI: Baker Books, 2005), 317.

9. Charles H. Spurgeon, *The Metropolitan Tabernacle Pulpit*, vol. 29 (Pasadena, TX: Pilgrim Publications, 1973), 363.

10. Piper, *What Jesus Demands from the World*, 207.

11. Oswald Chambers, *My Utmost for His Highest* (Grand Rapids, MI: Discovery House, 1992), December 7.

12. We can no more change our hearts than a "leopard his spots" (Jeremiah 13:23). See also John 6:44–45; Romans 9:16; 1 Corinthians 2:14.

13. For a detailed discussion of God's sovereignty and human responsibility, see Robert A. Peterson, *Election and Free Will: God's Gracious Choice and Our Responsibility* (Phillipsburg, NJ: P&R, 2001), 129.

14. Ibid., 143.

15. Piper, *What Jesus Demands from the World*, 40 (emphasis added).

Chapter 9: The Change That Brings Freedom

1. Arthur Bennett, ed., *The Valley of Vision: A Collection of Puritan Prayers & Devotions*, 167.

2. Thomas Watson, *The Doctrine of Repentance* (Carlisle, PA: Banner of Truth Trust, 1987), 18–58.

3. Ibid., 42.

4. Ibid., 47.

5. Charles H. Spurgeon, *Morning and Evening* (Wheaton, IL: Crossway Books, 2003), October 13.

6. Gregory Laughery, *Living Spirituality: Illuminating the Path* (Huémoz, Switzerland: Destinée S.A., 2006), 22.

7. Ibid., 23.

8. Ibid., 24.

9. Thomas Watson, *The Godly Man's Picture* (Carlisle, PA: Banner of Truth Trust, 1992), 146.

10. Oswald Chambers, *My Utmost for His Highest* (Grand Rapids, MI: Discovery House, 1992), January 30.

11. Robert A. Peterson, *Election and Free Will: God's Gracious Choice and Our Responsibility* (Phillipsburg, NJ: P & R, 2001), 131.

12. Watson, *The Doctrine of Repentance*, 77.

13. John Owen, *The Mortification of Sin* (Geanies House, Scotland: Christian Focus Publications, 2002), 92.

14. Michael Horton, *Christless Christianity* (Grand Rapids, MI: Baker Books, 2008), 74.

15. Chambers, *My Utmost for His Highest*, August 3.

16. Ibid.

Chapter 10: Spiritual Sexuality for Men

1. Arthur Bennett, ed., *The Valley of Vision: A Collection of Puritan Prayers & Devotions*, 282.

2. A full discussion on the issues of headship and submission goes far beyond the limits of this chapter and this book. Resources in the appendixes will guide you in a worthwhile, in-depth study.

3. John Piper, "A Vision of Biblical Complementarity: Manhood and Womanhood Defined according to the Bible," in *Recovering Biblical Manhood & Womanhood: A Response to Evangelical Feminism*, ed. John Piper and Wayne Grudem (Wheaton, IL: Crossway Books, 1991), 35, emphasis mine.

4. Piper and Grudem, *Recovering Biblical Manhood & Womanhood*, 38–42.

5. The exception is in a marriage that must endure physical, medical, and aging problems that can seriously hinder sexual intimacy. Some women are physiologically incapable of intercourse, and sometimes remain so even after surgery to correct the problem. For men, nerve damage can result in a male diabetic becoming impotent. Chronic illness, surgeries, and other medical issues along with aging can also present challenges to sexual intimacy. In such cases, always consult your physician for further advice. If you face these issues, work at alternative expressions of sexual and physical intimacy and always remain affectionate with your spouse.

6. Bennett, ed., *The Valley of Vision*, 258–59.

Chapter 11: Spiritual Sexuality for Women

1. Arthur Bennett, ed., *The Valley of Vision: A Collection of Puritan Prayers & Devotions*, 342.

2. Henri Nouwen, *Sabbatical Journey* (New York: Crossroad, 1998), 25.

3. John Piper, *This Momentary Marriage: A Parable of Permanence* (Wheaton, IL: Crossway Books, 2009), 159.

4. John Piper, *Spectacular Sins: And Their Global Purpose in the Glory of Christ* (Wheaton, IL: Crossway Books, 2008), 81.

5. Vern Sheridan Poythress, "The Church as Family: Why Male Leadership in the Family Requires Male Leadership in the Church," in *Recovering Biblical Manhood & Womanhood: A Response to Evangelical Feminism*, ed. John Piper and Wayne Grudem (Wheaton, IL: Crossway Books, 1991), 240.

6. John Piper, "A Vision of Biblical Complementarity: Manhood and Womanhood Defined according to the Bible," in *Recovering Biblical Manhood & Womanhood: A Response to Evangelical Feminism*, 46.

Chapter 12: The Seven Principles of Spiritual Sexuality

1. Arthur Bennett, ed., *The Valley of Vision: A Collection of Puritan Prayers & Devotions*, 265.

2. For a full description of this biblical view see the resources in the appendixes, and Garry Friesen's book *Decision Making and the Will of God* (Sisters, OR: Multnomah, 1980).

3. No one fully understands the mystery of how God's sovereignty and our responsibility work together in our lives. He must work, or there is no hope of sexual holiness. And we must make conscious choices to obey God. This is His plan for us, His divine will.

Chapter 13: Married and Intimate

1. Arthur Bennett, ed., *The Valley of Vision: A Collection of Puritan Prayers & Devotions*, 289.

2. Whatever your experience that now distorts your view of sexual intimacy, there is healing. Scripture is the final authority in all of life, including our sexuality. God's design for a married couple is that they be spiritual and sexual at the same time. Spirituality without sexual intimacy in marriage is dangerous for both the husband and the wife. Sexual intimacy without spirituality often leads to false intimacy. Sexual desire is not evil, it was designed by God for *both* men and women. Fault-finding, bitterness, and self-centeredness will always reduce that desire. Through the work of God in hearts that goes far beyond techniques, men and women have learned to enjoy the pleasure God intended in marriage.

   Much of counseling makes the mistake of treating the adulterer or sexual sinner alone. Wanting to protect the spouse from more hurt and pain, she is left out of the process entirely, or put on a different track. This is a significant mistake as it does not allow for the new expression of male leadership coming out of repentance to be immediately expressed. First Corinthians 7:3–5 teaches mutual obligation between a husband and a wife. It teaches us that leadership should not be selfish. If leadership is selfish in sexual intimacy, the mutual obligation breaks down, the wife feels obligated to perform, and ends up feeling like a sexual object. Women, and even counselors, end up thinking that men just want sex and that relationship means nothing to them.

Actually, that is not true. With every couple I've counseled grappling with this issue, every man will easily acknowledge that he would rather have a meaningful relationship and not just take sex from his wife. In fact, this is consistent with what a man is designed for sexually and relationally. If he acts like getting sex for himself is all he wants, he knows in his own mind he is being a fool, but in weakness he lets foolishness reign.

3. Noah Webster, *Noah Webster's First Edition of an American Dictionary of the English Language, 1828 Edition* (San Francisco: Foundation for American Christian Education, 1967).

Chapter 14: Joy in God—No Matter What Comes

1. Arthur Bennett, ed., *The Valley of Vision: A Collection of Puritan Prayers & Devotions*, 289.

2. Godly vulnerability is not codependency. It is pursuing a relationship for a purpose higher than ourselves. The purpose is for God's glory and to be an agent used of God in another person's life. To have that objective means that I will get involved at a level of deep concern for another person even if pain is the likely outcome.

3. See the stories of Jim Elliot and John and Betty Stam in the books *Through Gates of Splendor* (Tyndale, 1981) by Elizabeth Elliot, and *To Die Is Gain: The Triumph of John and Betty Stam* (Westminster Literature Resources, 2004) by Mrs. Howard Taylor.

4. Oswald Chambers, *My Utmost for His Highest* (Grand Rapids, MI: Discovery House, 1992), July 29.

5. Charles Spurgeon, *Morning and Evening* (Wheaton, IL: Crossway Books, 2003), May 22.

Chapter 15: The Next Sexual Revolution

1. Arthur Bennett, ed., *The Valley of Vision: A Collection of Puritan Prayers & Devotions*, 265.

2. For a definition, see appendix 3.

3. C. S. Lewis, *Mere Christianity* (New York: MacMillan, 1943), 174.

4. Review the following Scriptures for more details, and then study the entire New Testament to understand more about a godly life: Romans 12:1–13:14; Ephesians 4:17–6:20; Philippians 4:4–9; Colossians 3:5–4:6; 1 Peter 2:11–5:11.

5. Lewis, *Mere Christianity*, 95.

6. Bennett, ed., *The Valley of Vision*, 213.

Appendix 1: Masturbation: A Form of False Intimacy

1. Daniel R. Heimbach, *True Sexual Morality: Recovering Biblical Standards for a Culture in Crisis* (Wheaton, IL: Crossway Books, 2004), 222–23.

Appendix 2: Ten Things to Do When Your Spouse Is Unfaithful

1. This list is based on John Piper's "Eight Things to Do with Evil" in *Spectacular Sins: and Their Global Purpose in the Glory of Christ* (Wheaton, IL: Crossway Books, 2008), 50.

Appendix 3: What Does It Mean to "Get It"?

1. Harry W. Schaumburg, *Brief Intensive Counseling Manual: A Guided Study Program*, 2002.

Appendix 5: A Different View on Divorce

1. John Piper, *This Momentary Marriage: A Parable of Permanence* (Wheaton, IL: Crossway Books, 2009), 160.

2. Ibid., 174.

Appendix 6: A Call to Modesty

1. C. J. Mahaney, ed., *Worldliness: Resisting the Seduction of a Fallen World* (Wheaton, IL: Crossway Books, 2008), 173.

2. John MacArthur, *1 Timothy*, The MacArthur New Testament Commentary (Chicago: Moody, 1995), 80–81.

3. C. J. Mahaney, ed., *Worldliness*, 174.

4. To read Carolyn Mahaney's complete "Modesty Heart Check," see *Worldliness: Resisting the Seduction of a Fallen World*, 173–76.

Acknowledgments

Providentially, God has used four major factors to make this book possible.

First and foremost is the Lord Himself. I can't write without Him. I have nothing to say unless by His grace He puts within me the spiritual wisdom and knowledge. I believe that there is nothing in the pages of this book worth reading that isn't the fruit of God working in my heart. He deserves all the glory. If there is anything I've written that distracts from His will and purpose, it is my own foolishness and I ask for the Lord's mercy and beg your forgiveness. Moody Publishers gave me six months to write this book, but my Father in heaven gave me more than sixty years to get ready. I believe with all my heart and mind that God mercifully shapes us for His purpose and glory, not our own. There are many things that happen in life that we never anticipate. In my wildest dreams I would never have imagined how God's loving discipline would batter me into shape to bring me to a place where I could write and speak on such a crucial and sensitive topic. To God be the glory forever and ever!

The second factor is Bruce Nygren. I knew I wanted to write another book. Little did I know God in His sovereignty would ignore my thoughts and bring Bruce Nygren back across my path with the better idea. He believed I was to write a new book on the same subject as my first book. Frankly, his idea did not appeal to me until we sat down to discuss the project. Bruce not only believed there was a need to write such a book, he helped me form the structure, and then worked to sell the idea to Moody Publishers. Finally, he added his creativity and gifted editing skills to reshape the first draft. I appreciate all the time and effort he has put into this project. The Lord will continue to use you for His purpose in your next assignment.

Third, there is only one human with whom I am the most intimate, and I am the one who is blessed. She makes everything I do, say, or write have extra purpose and value. This book is fittingly dedicated to Rosemary, my wife of forty years. She is my best friend, lover, and helper. It is her tender love, consistent faithfulness, and never-ending passion that I find my greatest human delight. As all good servants of the Lord, she has no idea the imprint she has made, not only on me, but on this book. Without her I would have no credibility to write about spirituality and sexuality.

Fourth, there are countless names and faces of hundreds upon hundreds of men and women who have sat in my office overwhelmed with the horror of their sexual sin and staggered by the pain of betrayal. They came seeking hope, and many found help. All of you have no idea how His divine design of our interactions has been used to shape my life and my thinking about spirituality and sexuality. I'm still learning from you. Without you opening to me the deepest recesses of your private lives, your persistent questions, your eagerness to know God, and then allowing me to see the grace of God work in your hearts, I would have little to write. To the alumni of Biblical Intensive Counseling, thank you for what you have given me and for your prayers that made this book possible. May each one of you continue to struggle well.

I want to also thank Paul Santhouse for his support. Little did we know several years ago where our discussion over lunch would lead us. There have been some twists and turns in terms of writing and publishing a book and you played a big part in making this one happen.

I enjoy reading, and have read many books on many subjects, and therefore I am influenced by a host of writers and thinkers. Three sources are the most influential at this time in my life. John Piper guides my thinking and often confirms my own fledgling thoughts. Oswald Chambers has challenged me daily for as far back as I can remember. The list of dead guys, whom I prefer to read, grows, and most of them are Puritans.

Thanks to Brian Bunn and Brian Chronister, two good friends, for your willingness to read my manuscript and give me valuable feedback.

I feel like the pilot who gets to fly the airplane. But without a crew, dispatcher, gate agents, baggage handlers, and mechanics, the plane doesn't take off. A special thanks to Madison Trammel and Chris Reese for all of their help and editorial work. Thank you to all the staff at Moody Publishers for getting this book off the ground.

CLOSE CALLS

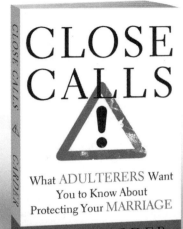

ISBN-13: 978-0-8024-4211-6

Never say never—your marriage may be the most vulnerable when you think it is adultery-proof. Dave Carder, counselor, and author of the bestselling *Torn Asunder* (over 100,000 in print), is a sought-after expert on issues of adultery. Carder reveals what adulterers learned the hard way—and what they want the rest of us to know. Includes charts and assessments.

TORN ASUNDER

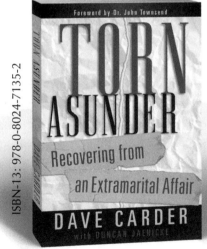

ISBN-13: 978-0-8024-7135-2

Infidelity is at crisis level even within the church. No marriage is immune despite apparent moral convictions. Dave Carder wrote *Torn Asunder* to offer couples hope, healing, and encouragement in the face of adultery. He divides his book into first helping readers understand extramarital affairs and then offering healing for marriages dealing with this betrayal. Excellent resource for pastors, leaders, and laypeople.

1-800-678-8812 • MOODYPUBLISHERS.COM

Porn Nation

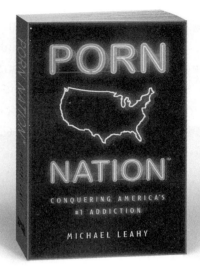

ISBN-13: 978-0-8024-8125-2

It's a $100B a year industry worldwide. Even bigger when you consider the fact that porn is now the norm in our mainstream media. But have you ever stopped to think about why, when it comes to porn, we just can't seem to get enough? Enter Michael Leahy, a guy who spent over 30 years as a recreational user of pornography. That is until he discovered what many experts refer to as "the crack cocaine of sexual addiction"—Internet porn. What happened next would change everything, not just for Michael and his family but for all of us living in this porn nation.

Porn at Work

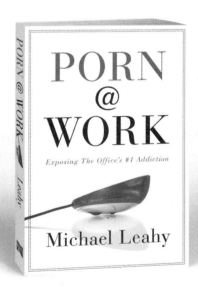

ISBN-13: 978-0-8024-8129-0

Speaking from personal experience and drawing on several years' worth of research surveys, author Michael Leahy presents the facts about our porn-saturated world in the place where we spend the most time: our jobs. The latest era of workplace connectivity has given rise to a whole new level of office efficiency, but it has also opened the door to all kinds of potential dangers and temptations. Lost productivity and litigation risks are where the errant click-throughs generally lead. Don't fall into the trap! Porn doesn't have to be the norm.

NORTHFIELD
PUBLISHING

1-800-678-8812 • MOODYPUBLISHERS.COM